RICH

A Biblical Perspective On

TITHING
FAITHFULLY

Going From Obedience
to Blessing

abc

Book Publishing

Published by
ABC Book Publishing

AbcBookPublishing.com
Printed in U.S.A.
A Biblical Perspective On Tithing Faithfully:
Going From Obedience to Blessing
© Copyright 2008 by Richard A. Brott

Layout and Cover Design by Metanoia Publishing, Jakarta-Indonesia

ISBN: 1-60185-001-8
ISBN (EAN): 978-1-60185-001-0

About The Author

Rich Brott holds a Bachelor of Science degree in Business and Economics and a Master of Business Administration.

Rich has served in an executive position of some very successful businesses. He has functioned on the board of directors for churches, businesses, and charities and served on a college advisory board. Rich has traveled to more than 25 countries on teaching assignments and business concerns.

Rich Brott has authored over thirty-five books including:

- *5 Simple Keys to Financial Freedom*
- *10 Life-Changing Attitudes That Will Make You a Financial Success*
- *15 Biblical Responsibilities Leading to Financial Wisdom*
- *30 Biblical Principles for Managing Your Money*
- *35 Keys to Financial Independence*
- *A Biblical Perspective on Giving Generously*
- *A Biblical Perspective on Tithing & Giving*
- *A Biblical Perspective on Tithing Faithfully*
- *Achieving Financial Alignment*
- *Activating Your Personal Faith to Receive*
- *All the Financial Scriptures in the Bible*
- *Basic Principles for Business Success*
- *Basic Principles for Developing Personal and Business Vision*
- *Basic Principles for Managing a Successful Business*
- *Basic Principles for Maximizing Your Personal Cash Flow*
- *Basic Principles for Starting a Successful Business*

- *Basic Principles of Conservative Investing*
- *Biblical Principles for Achieving Personal Success*
- *Biblical Principles for Becoming Debt Free*
- *Biblical Principles for Building a Successful Business*
- *Biblical Principles for Financial Success - Student Workbook*
- *Biblical Principles for Financial Success - Teacher Workbook*
- *Biblical Principles for Personal Evangelism*
- *Biblical Principles for Releasing Financial Provision*
- *Biblical Principles for Staying Out of Debt*
- *Biblical Principles for Success in Personal Finance*
- *Biblical Principles That Create Success Through Productivity*
- *Business, Occupations, Professions & Vocations In the Bible*
- *Family Finance Handbook*
- *Family Finance Student Workbook*
- *Family Finance Teacher Workbook*
- *How to Receive Prosperity and Provision*
- *Prosperity Has a Purpose*
- *Public Relations for the Local Church*
- *Successful Time Management*

He and his wife Karen, have been married for 36 years. Rich Brott resides in Portland, Oregon, with his wife, three children, son-in-law and granddaughter.

Dedication

This book is dedicated to every person who has made the decision to follow the tithing principles of God's Word. By choosing the pathway of obedience, they will not have to worry about their future. As promised in Scripture, God will...

1. Pass the test.

Bring the whole tithe into the storehouse, that there may be food in my house. Test me in this," says the LORD Almighty,

2. Pour out blessing.

"and see if I will not throw open the floodgates of heaven and pour out so much blessing that you will not have room enough for it.

3. Protect the works of your labor.

I will prevent pests from devouring your crops, and the vines in your fields will not cast their fruit," says the LORD Almighty.

Malachi 3:10-12 (NIV)

Table of Contents

A Biblical Perspective on Tithing Faithfully

Going From Obedience to Blessing

Introduction

This book is about becoming a faithful tither. It is about doing the right thing. It is about returning the tenth to God. It is about stepping out in obedience and learning to walk in biblical principles. It is also about finding out that when we obey the Scriptures, we will also be able to partake in the blessings of God.

What you care about you invest in. If you invest your provision with the things that God is interested in, your attitude will be the same. You will be interested in the ministry advance of your local church and will pray for the expansion of His Kingdom locally and globally. Note that Jesus did not say to have nothing, or enjoy nothing. Nor does he imply any kind of a sin. Christ is saying to us not to get too tied to these things.

Be a conduit, not a dam. It is not about what you have, but what has you. If you center your life around your things, and base your living upon your possessions, you will surely be disappointed.

Don't base your life, your future, your well-being, or your happiness on the things you have accumulated. Instead be sure that you lay up for yourself the real treasures, the ones that will be of eternal value.

Chapter 1

It's About Your Heart, Not Your Money!

*T*he topic of tithing on your increase always relates to your entire life and all that you are concerned with. It's not strictly a financial issue. We have much to give that is far more valuable than money. We have our time, our commitment, our attitude, our gifting, our energy, our service, our talent, our assets, our devotion and our entire life. Yet in all that we have to offer, our attitude toward our finances does play an important role and affects the other areas of our life.

When it comes to the non-monetary resources we have, such as our personal time, biblical stewardship is not about twisting arms and attempting to persuade people to volunteer for needed services. Rather it is about helping people recognize their God-given talents and abilities and helping them move into the giftings they have been blessed with.

Once talents have been discovered and giftings acknowledged, it becomes the job of the church to figure out how those personal gifts can be utilized. It's not about volunteerism, but it is about gift mobilization.

Biblical stewardship is not about giving a lot of money just so the church can function in its community role. Yes, the church does need financing for its operational needs and vision mandate. But your role in receiving the blessings of God is all about you keeping only a needed portion of God's blessing and returning a large portion of the blessing so that others can be blessed as well. We should become resourceful and efficient stewards of all the possessions God has sent our way.

Our culture and society have sold us a bill of goods. They teach us that in order to be happy, we have to have certain things. But we must resist the world's view of wealth, happiness, and possessions. We don't have to have it all! We don't have to wear just the right clothes, drive that certain brand of car, have the latest model available, buy a bigger home, possess the latest digital camera, and carry a dozen credit cards in our wallet.

We must not allow our culture to dictate to us its worldview of what our lives should consist of. Our society should not be allowed to design our lifestyle, nor should it tell us what success is and what the picture of affluence should look like. Success is doing what God wants done.

Wealth is having only what you need to exist. A rich man or woman is one who has one penny more than he or she needs. Wealth is more than money. It is having a local church that inspires you to draw close to God. It is having a loving spouse and the blessing of children. Wealth is enjoying great health and great relationships. Wealth is having good friends. Wealth is receiving salvation and God's gift of eternal life with Him.

Chapter 2

The Money Decisions of
4 Bible Characters

It has always been fascinating to me that on the face of the coin and currency of the United States money, it reads, "In God We Trust." Although it seems that as a nation we may not be practicing what we preach in this regard, my prayer is that we will one day return to the faith of our founding fathers.

If I could sum up the purpose and content of this entire book on tithing faithfully, it would be this simple yet profound statement, "In God We Trust." If in your personal life, both successes and failures, you could live out this truth, the end result would be a life lived with supernatural blessing and provision.

Yet for many, this reality is not understood, nor accepted. When it comes to managing the finances God has sent their way, instead of becoming wise stewards, they have chosen to become like small children in a candy store; spending the surplus to gratify their own wants and desires. For them the more appropriate description of their attitude toward money would be, "In You I Trust."

JOB 1:21
"Naked I came from my mother's womb, and naked I will depart. The LORD gave and the LORD has taken away; may the name of the LORD be praised."

Not that money is unimportant—it is important, and sustains our livelihood. If spent in the right way, on the right things and in the right places it can do a lot of good. But God places great importance on the methods we use to make that money. Proverbs 15:6 notes, "The house of the righteous contains great treasure, but the income of the wicked brings them trouble."

You see, what we are is far more important than what we possess. Shedding all sense of right and wrong and morals for the sake of money is the most foolish thing a person can do. Yet, men and women get involved all the time in things that are not honest and respectable because of greed for material things.

When it comes to personal possessions, money and wealth, you cannot take it with you but you CAN send it on ahead. Bottom line is this: what you keep, you will lose, but what you give away, you will gain. After all, when is the last time that you saw a hearse pulling a U-Haul trailer behind it on the way to the cemetery?

In the Gospels we read about four different individuals who all faced provision issues that required decisions about money. Let's take a look at each person and the life-changing / eternity effecting decisions they made.

The Ruthless Rich Man
Luke 16:19-31

"There was a rich man who was dressed in purple and fine linen and lived in luxury every day. At his gate was laid a beggar named Lazarus, covered with sores and longing to eat what fell from the rich man's table. Even the dogs came and licked his sores. The time came when the beggar died and the angels carried him to Abraham's side. The rich man also died and was buried. In hell, where he was in torment, he looked up and saw Abraham far away, with Lazarus by his side. So he called to him, 'Father Abraham, have pity on me and send Lazarus to dip the tip of his finger in water and cool my tongue, because I am in agony in this fire.'

But Abraham replied, 'Son, remember that in your lifetime you received your good things, while Lazarus received bad things, but now he is comforted here and you are in agony. And besides all this, between us and you a great chasm has been fixed, so that those who want to go from here to you cannot, nor can anyone cross over from there to us.' He answered, 'Then I beg you, father, send Lazarus to my father's house, for I have five brothers. Let him warn them, so that they will not also come to this place of torment.' "Abraham replied, 'They have Moses and the Prophets; let them listen to them.'

'No, father Abraham,' he said, 'but if someone from the dead goes to them, they will repent.' "He said to him, 'If they do not listen to Moses and the Prophets, they will not be convinced even if someone rises from the dead.'"

17

The poor beggar by the name of Lazarus was left to die at the gate of the rich man without food to nourish him and keep him alive. All he wanted was mere crumbs that fell from his table, yet the rich man who lived in luxury refused to come to his aid or meet his need for mere survival.

The Foolish Rich Man
Luke 12:16-21

"And he told them this parable: "The ground of a certain rich man produced a good crop. He thought to himself, 'What shall I do? I have no place to store my crops.' Then he said, 'This is what I'll do. I will tear down my barns and build bigger ones, and there I will store all my grain and my goods. And I'll say to myself, "You have plenty of good things laid up for many years. Take life easy; eat, drink and be merry." '

But God said to him, 'You fool! This very night your life will be demanded from you. Then who will get what you have prepared for yourself?' This is how it will be with anyone who stores up things for himself but is not rich toward God."

This man apparently thought he would live forever…or at least a very long time. After storing up wealth for a long time (hoarding) he was planning to take his ease. Luke 12:15 instructs us to be on guard against every form of greed. It says that even when we have abundance, our lives are not to be caught up in our possessions.

Much of western culture is centered around things and possessions that money can buy. Christian culture in the West is not immune to its influence. It's not that we are necessarily in love with money, but certainly we could say that we are enticed, maybe entrapped by what we know that money can do for us. Of course we do live in this society and in this world's system, and we should not be so unwise as to think that we are immune from it altogether.

The Bible has a lot to say about material goods and our desire for them. The Apostle Paul suggests that contentment is a very powerful value to guide us. Then he reminds us that we came into this world with nothing and will depart in the same way. He suggests that we should be happy when we have food to eat and clothes to wear. He notes that people who desire to get rich quickly often fall into temptation fulfilling harmful desires that lead to ruin and destruction.

The Greedy Rich Young Ruler
Matthew 19:16-24

"Now a man came up to Jesus and asked, "Teacher, what good thing must I do to get eternal life?"

"Why do you ask me about what is good?" Jesus replied. "There is only One who is good. If you want to enter life, obey the commandments." "Which ones?" the man inquired. Jesus replied, "'Do not murder, do not commit adultery, do not steal, do not give false testimony, honor your father and mother,' and 'love your neighbor as yourself.'" "All these I have kept," the young man said. "What do I still lack?"

Jesus answered, "If you want to be perfect, go, sell your possessions and give to the poor, and you will have treasure in heaven. Then come, follow me." When the young man heard this, he went away sad, because he had great wealth. Then Jesus said to his disciples, "I tell you the truth, it is hard for a rich man to enter the kingdom of heaven. Again I tell you, it is easier for a camel to go through the eye of a needle than for a rich man to enter the kingdom of God."

So many people today are on a quest to accumulate possessions and wealth. It is hard for all of us to be content with what we have when the world's entire system is geared toward making us unhappy with everything we have and desirous of everything we don't have. From advertising to attitude, we face a discontented culture.

How much money do we want to be content? Usually just a little bit more. Money cannot buy contentment or happiness. It is very hard for us to be satisfied with what we do have, but we need to strive for contentment and contend for happiness. There is certainly nothing wrong with making money, so long as making money does not violate the laws of our land and the principles of God's Word.

The all-for-me and none-for-others way of man's thinking is immoral. The person of principle who subscribes to the values of the Bible will be a good steward who obeys the law of giving. This person will find happiness in exact proportion to the degree that he gives. He will be content with his life and all that it affords.

The story of Matthew 19 is the history of one who was a great young man; a good man; and it seems a principled man. He belonged to the ruling class of his time in history. But even in his culture, he was apparently influenced by a society of peers involved in hoarding finances.

Because the quantity of his possessions and personal wealth was substantial, he made a choice to hang on to what he had. Instead of being the conduit that God intended, the receiving vessel thought it all belonged to him. The love of money representing personal greed kept him from following Christ.

The lesson learned here can really be summed up in the form of a few questions. Are you satisfied with temporary treasure on earth, or are you preparing for eternal treasures in the life hereafter? Do you hold money, wealth and possessions for the purpose of blessing others, or does the money, wealth and assets that God has trusted you with, have a hold on you?

The Compassionate Rich Man
Luke 10:30-37

"In reply Jesus said: "A man was going down from Jerusalem to Jericho, when he fell into the hands of robbers. They stripped him of his clothes, beat him and went away, leaving him half dead. A priest happened to be going down the same road, and when he saw the man, he passed by on the other side. So too, a Levite, when he came to the place and saw him, passed by on the other side. But a Samaritan, as he traveled, came where the man was; and when he saw him, he took pity on him. He went to him and bandaged his wounds, pouring on oil and wine. Then he put the man on his own donkey, took him to an inn and took care of him. The next day he took out two silver coins and gave them to the innkeeper. 'Look after him,' he said, 'and when I return, I will reimburse you for any extra expense you may have.'

"Which of these three do you think was a neighbor to the man who fell into the hands of robbers?" The expert in the law replied, "The one who had mercy on him." Jesus told him, "Go and do likewise."

Better known to us in story as the Good Samaritan, this person used the resources trusted to him by God to help someone in need. The story of the Good Samaritan is the story of the integrity of a steward. Stewardship means that God owns you and is counting on you to become an instrument through which He can love and save the world. It's as simple as that! If you cannot offer yourself as a channel of God's wealth, how can He bless your life? The bottom line in stewardship is not money or a block of time, but your entire life and how you respond to those in need whose paths you cross.

Nothing happens in the economy of God until you give something away. It is a universal law of God. Paul very appropriately reminds us: "Remember this: Whoever sows sparingly will also reap sparingly, and whoever sows generously will also reap generously" (II Corinthians 9:6).

Giving is the trigger for God's financial miracles. When you give to the Kingdom of God, it will be given back to you. But where will it come from? Who will give to you? Will God cause money to float down from heaven so that your needs will be met? No. The Bible says, "shall men give into your ....(life)."

This is how the cycle of blessing works. When you give to God, He in turn causes others to give to you. Perhaps it will be in the form of new customers to your business, new products to sell, and so on. When God owns your business, He will make sure it prospers.

The Scriptures illustrate that giving of one's own things is an evidence of God's grace in a person's life. (II Corinthians 8:4-7) Because 100 percent of what is received comes from God, we are responsible to use it wisely and in accordance with God's will. Like every other area of stewardship, God is interested in the whole picture, not just a percentage. What a person does with all his treasure is important to God.

The Good Samaritan was a trustee of God's provision. The person who takes stewardship seriously will regard his or her life, talents, strength and money as a trust from God. Trustees have specific responsibilities. They are charged with "holding property in trust" for someone else. Scriptural principles give us clues as to how we can trust God with our money and our entire life.

24

1 Timothy 6:17-19

"Command those who are rich in this present world not to be arrogant nor to put their hope in wealth, which is so uncertain, but to put their hope in God, who richly provides us with everything for our enjoyment. Command them to do good, to be rich in good deeds, and to be generous and willing to share. In this way they will lay up treasure for themselves as a firm foundation for the coming age, so that they may take hold of the life that is truly life."

Matthew 6:19-21

"Do not store up for yourselves treasures on earth, where moth and rust destroy, and where thieves break in and steal. But store up for yourselves treasures in heaven, where moth and rust do not destroy, and where thieves do not break in and steal. For where your treasure is, there your heart will be also."

What we care about we invest in. If we invest our provision with the things that God is interested in, our attitude will be the same. We will be interested in the ministry advance of our local church and will pray for the expansion of His Kingdom locally and globally. Note that Jesus is not saying to have nothing, or enjoy nothing. Nor does he imply any kind of a sin. Christ is saying to us not to get too tied to these things.

Be a conduit, not a dam. It is not about what we have, but what has us. If we center our life around our things, base our living upon our possessions, we will surely be disappointed. Don't base your life, your future, your well-being, or your happiness on the things you have accumulated. Instead, be sure that you lay up for yourself the real treasures, the ones that will be of eternal value. A couple of parting thought-provoking questions for your consideration.

1. Where are you placing your treasures?

2. Do you identify with the ruthless, the foolish, the greedy or the compassionate use of God's blessing?

3. Will you be a conduit or channel through which blessings surge or a dam that stops the flow of the blessing of God?

These are very candid, tough questions; were you satisfied with your answer?

Chapter 3

12 Principles of Tithing

$\mathcal{I}$t is such a blessing to be a tither! Your tithe is the first part of your giving commitment. When you give with joy and give with all your heart, you are not concerned so much with giving an amount of minimal acceptance. But tithing of our increase is a very real minimum giving opportunity necessary even for this generation.

> **GENESIS 28:20–22**
> *Then Jacob made a vow, saying, "If God will be with me and will watch over me on this journey I am taking and will give me food to eat and clothes to wear so that I return safely to my father's house, then the LORD will be my God and this stone that I have set up as a pillar will be God's house, and of all that you give me I will give you a tenth."*

Early in biblical history we see a picture of Jacob, a man who promised God that he would return a tenth of all his increase. Jacob was beginning a journey, apparently leaving his family for a period of time, making his bed under the stars. God came to him in a dream, promising him great blessings in the future, which of course He gave. Jacob promised the tenth, as he understood the principle of the tenth.

There are many reasons for tithing.

1.
God is training us to be faithful stewards in handling money.

People who do not pay a tithe, or tenth, of their income often have poor financial habits that leave them broke soon after payday. Tithing teaches us to pay that which we owe first. Our financial obligation to God is first priority. When He blesses us with increase, He expects us to give a minimum of 10 percent as a tithe into the "storehouse," which in definition is our local church. We should be cheerful givers! We should give out of our abundance. We should give out of our love. And we should give to meet the needs of those who do not have and find themselves in lack.

2.
God is teaching us the principle concerning the cycle of money.

We reap what we sow, and God is training us to plant some "seed money" in tithing so that He will have cause to abundantly bless us. In the same way that just one seed can multiply itself many times over, so it is with money. Certainly our investments should include investing in God's work.

3.
The tithe belongs to God (Leviticus 27:30).

It is already His, and if we withhold it we are robbing Him (Malachi 3:8). Robbery is taking that which belongs to another for personal use, either by fraud or violence. It is not only taking what is not yours, but also keeping back for yourself what belongs to someone else. One-tenth of your income belongs to God, and failure to pay that debt is robbery.

When we rob God, we permit something to have stronger power over us than His will does. When we retain God's money in our treasuries, we will find it a losing proposition.

How can a person not pay tithes? Can we afford to be so selfish as not to give God His small part, especially when it was all His to begin with? Can we hold a tight fist in the face of God, who has freely given us all things (Romans 8:32)?

4.
Tithing is commanded.

Malachi 3:10 says, "Bring ye all the tithes into the storehouse." Tithing, as established by Abraham, involves giving 10 percent of one's earnings.

5.
Abraham tithed before the law of Moses.

The first biblical record of tithing is found in Genesis 14. Abram's nephew, Lot, was taken captive in a battle between some kings and their armies. When Abram set out to rescue him, not only was he successful, but he also brought back a large amount of spoils. Genesis 14:11–20 records this event.

This Old Testament account of the first mention of tithing indicates that the spoils belonged to Abram by right of conquest. Abram has been called the "father of the faithful" (Romans 4), and his life is exemplary to us today, his faith a prototype for all believers. In this passage we are told that Melchizedek was the "priest of God Most High."

Verse 19 notes that Abram was also "of the most high God" (KJV). And we are told that the most high God is "possessor of heaven and earth" (v. 19, KJV). Apparently, tithing in this context was a direct acknowledgment of the sovereignty and lordship of God over all the earth.

Giving God back a tenth of what is already His anyway was a way of acknowledging God's ownership of the entire earth's wealth. Haggai 2:8 declares, "The silver is mine, and the gold is mine, saith the LORD of hosts" (KJV).

If God cannot trust you with the first portion, how can He give you future destiny?

6.
The New Testament recounts the first tithe.

Hebrews 7:1–19 records the same story as Genesis 14. This is the last direct reference to tithing in the New Testament, and it seems interesting to me that it also refers to the first reference found in the Old Testament.

Abraham gave tithes to Melchizedek long before the Mosaic law was given by God at Mount Sinai. Abraham honored the Most High God by freely giving from a loving, grateful heart. It was a true act of worship. Abraham's giving was not based on the law but on a grateful response to God's grace. You can give without loving, but you cannot love without giving!

7.
A "tithe" is a tenth.

The "tithe" simply means the "tenth." A tenth is 10 percent. A ratio of one to ten is easy to remember and easy to figure—much like our decimal system today. It seems natural and logical to divide things into tens.

· Tithing is scriptural.
· Tithing is systematic.
· Tithing is simple.
· Tithing is successful.
· Tithing is right.

God has ordained that the use of money is related to spiritual values. The only way to get our treasures into heaven is to put them into something that is going to heaven. Cattle, lands, stocks, bonds, and houses will not make it to heaven.

Only men, women, boys, and girls of all color are going to heaven. By exchanging our earthly possessions and money into the saving of souls, we will take our acquired wealth with us to an eternal home.

8.
The tithe is the first part.

The tithe is the first part of our income. It is to be set apart before the rent, before the bills, and before we go shopping because it belongs to God and He must come first in our lives. We are to give it to the Lord as a token of gratefulness, recognizing that He is the originator of all our income.

DEUTERONOMY 26:10
"And now, behold, I have brought the firstfruits of the land which you, O LORD, have given me." Then you shall set it before the LORD your God, and worship before the LORD your God."

9.
Tithing does away with hit-and-miss methods of giving.

If a person is truly tithing, it is a systematic giving of 10 percent of all earnings to the Lord's work. If we earn ten dollars, one dollar of it is given back to God, and we are allowed to live on the remaining 90 percent. Some may think that if they gave God an occasional tenth, this would be enough. But people cannot be counted as tithers unless they consistently give a tenth.

The Bible teaches that tithing is to be the minimum of one's giving, not the maximum.

Just because one gives a tenth does not necessarily mean he has fulfilled his stewardship responsibility to God. We are to put God first and show that He is most important to us by tithing the firstfruits of our income. First means that which is before anything else in the order of time, before all others in place and in consideration.

Traditionally, the "firstfruits" is the fruit or produce first matured and collected in season. All we are, all we possess, and all we earn are equally the gifts of God. We are to acknowledge God as giver of all good things, which are the support and comfort of our natural lives, and therefore we are to give to God our first and our best.

I don't know how the Lord does it, but I have seen It work in my life over and over. I've seen the Lord bless the nine-tenths after the tithe until it went further than the full amount would have if I had withheld the first tenth.

When we give God our firstfruits, He multiplies it back to us many times over.

10.
Jesus Christ endorsed tithing.

Jesus Christ did not repeal the law concerning tithing; instead, He endorsed it. Tithe paying was a general practice during the time of Christ. In the New Testament, the term tithe(s) is found ten times. The sect that was strictest concerning tithing was the Pharisees. In order to be admitted into the fellowship of the Pharisees, one was obligated to pay his tithe. He was obligated to tithe to the treasury what he bought, what he sold, and what he ate.

Three of the references are found in the Gospels. Jesus faced the question of tithing. If He had not been a tither, this would have been one of the first complaints of the Pharisees. They continually watched His every word and action, seeking to find fault with Him, but they never once pointed to a lack of tithing.

The fact that Jesus Christ was admitted into the homes of the Pharisees for meals is evidence that He was a tither. Luke 11:37 says, "As he spake, a certain Pharisee besought him to dine with him: and he went in, and sat down to meat" (KJV). It was definitely against the vow of a Pharisee to be the host of an outsider. In Luke 18:22,

Christ did not offer disapproval to the Pharisee who said, "I give tithes of all that I possess," nor was He finding fault in his tithe paying. Jesus was condemning this attitude of self-righteousness and egotism.

11.
Becoming a tither.

If you have not been tithing, according to Scripture you have been robbing God. Thankfully, we can walk in the promises of God. One such promise is that God will forgive us when we confess our sins. God is ready to forgive you today of any unrighteousness on your part with regards to the tithe. He is ready to pour out blessing on your life as He opens His storehouse to us.

1 JOHN 1:9
"If we confess our sins, He is faithful and just to forgive us our sins and to cleanse us from all unrighteousness."

God has issued an invitation to prove the Lord's promises, to test Him with our tithe. He virtually offers a guaranteed direct and abundant return on your investment into His kingdom. This return comes in the form of His blessing. When we tithe, we can contend for God's promises.

12.
Promises to the tither.

There are many promises in God's Word for those who tithe faithfully. The command to tithe in Malachi 3:10 is followed up by some great promises. As we tithe, the Lord's response is to open for us the windows of heaven. Verse 11 says that He pours out for us "such blessing that there will not be room enough to receive it"! Tithing activates this great blessing in our lives.

This verse goes on to promise that God will rebuke the devourer for our sakes so that the fruit of our ground will not be destroyed and the vine will bear fruit for us in the field. When we tithe, God personally goes to bat for us against the enemy of our soul with regards to our finances.

We can be sure that when we sow, we will bear fruit. He causes our ground and fields to prosper. Who wouldn't like to see the hand of God at work in our workplace as we watch in wonder at how God causes the fruit of our labor to prosper?

When the blessing of God falls on us in such a mighty way, we can be sure that it won't go unnoticed. Malachi 3:12 shares the result of this great blessing: "'And all nations will call you blessed, For you will be a delightful land,' Says the LORD of hosts." How exciting that this blessing will not only be noticeable to us, but also to our coworkers, neighbors, and families.

PROVERBS 28:20
A faithful man will abound with blessings, but he who hastens to be rich will not go unpunished.

35

As we are faithful and test God in this area, let's trust Him to fulfill His promises. Be abundantly blessed!

Chapter 4

41 Questions About Tithing

What Is Tithing?

A tithe is a debt owed. It refers to the tenth of our increase that already belongs to God. It is not ours to keep. We pay it as we would any other debt. Debts are paid, not given. There are consequences to unpaid debt. In the context of tithing, the inaction of unpaid debt results in the action of "robbery." In Scripture, the only way man can rob God is by not returning the tenth that is already His to begin with.

> **MALACHI 3:8**
> *Will a man rob God? Yet you rob me. "But you ask, 'How do we rob you?' In tithes and offerings."*

One of the biggest tests in the walk of many people is the command to tithe. It is a spiritual test. God owns everything according to the Bible. And anything that we have by way of possessions is simply because God allows us to have them.

Exodus 19:5
Now therefore, if ye will obey my voice indeed, and keep my covenant, then ye shall be a peculiar treasure unto me above all people: for all the earth is mine. (KJV)

Psalm 50:12
If I were hungry I would not tell you, for the world is mine, and all that is in it. Although the Lord already owns everything, He does allow us to keep a significant part of the fruit of our labor. He gives us the greater portion—the 90 percent. And with our obedience, God promises to bless us when we tithe! When you tithe, He will make the 90 percent stretch further than the whole 100 percent should you keep it in disobedience.

What Is the Premise for Tithing?

The Old Testament believers were required to give a specific amount of money in order to meet the needs of the ministry, the poor, etc. While the New Testament does not specifically mention the tithe as a directive, 2 Corinthians 8:3 does direct us to give as we are able and even above and beyond. Jesus' view on giving was even more radical than tithing! He did not want us to be bound by material things and even said that we should sell our possessions and give all to the poor.

Luke told us to accumulate our treasures in heaven, where they would be safe from moths and thieves. When you look closely, the tithe of 10 percent seems like a minimum giving guideline in the New Testament. The new did not replace the old, but it increased and expanded the giving possibilities.

When Was the First Tithe Given?

Abraham tithed before the law of Moses. The first biblical record of tithing is found in Genesis 14. Abram's nephew, Lot, was taken captive in a battle between some kings and their armies. When Abram set out to rescue him, not only was he successful, but he also brought back a large amount of spoils. Genesis 14:11–20 records this event.

Giving God back a tenth of what was already His was a way of acknowledging God's ownership of the entire earth's wealth. Haggai 2:8 declares, "The silver is mine, and the gold is mine, saith the LORD of hosts" (KJV). Long before the time of Moses, the dedication of the tenth to God was recognized as a duty. It was consecrated and set apart for special purposes.

Was Tithing Commanded in the Patriarchal Days?

Yes, please note the following Scriptures on this topic:

GENESIS 14:20
"And blessed be God Most High, who delivered your enemies into your hand." Then Abram gave him a tenth of everything.

GENESIS 28:22
And this stone that I have set up as a pillar will be God's house, and of all that you give me I will give you a tenth.

LEVITICUS 27:30
A tithe of everything from the land, whether grain from the soil or fruit from the trees, belongs to the LORD; it is holy to the LORD.

LEVITICUS 27:32
The entire tithe of the herd and flock—every tenth animal that passes under the shepherd's rod—will be holy to the LORD.

When you say to "tithe," how much is that?

The tithe simply means the "tenth." A tenth is 10 percent. A ratio of one to ten is easy to remember and easy to figure—much like our decimal system today. It seems natural and logical to divide things into tens. God intended that the use of money be related to spiritual values.

How should I calculate and pay my tithes?

Your first calculation is to figure your increase. That might be from a paycheck, bonuses, or the sale of some property. When you think "increase," it becomes easier to figure God's tithe. After figuring out how much increase you have received, calculate the tithe, or the tenth. God's portion of your increase is 10 percent. You keep the 90 percent, you pay the 10 percent.

Is the tithe always money?

No! Money is certainly a necessary part of it (i.e. our employment paychecks, bonuses, etc.). However, our "increase" is often more than money. It could be non-monetary increases such as real estate, stocks, or simply vegetables grown in our garden.

When should I tithe?

You should tithe just as soon as you receive the increase. In the New Testament, the apostle Paul laid out a plan to the saints in Galatia and also to the Corinthian church. This was meant to bring some order and consistency to their giving. Simply put, he told them to hold out their tithe whenever they were paid and to present it on the first day of the week set aside for their worship. This was not only meant for continuity and regularity, but also for simplicity and convenience for them as they gathered for worship on the first day of the week.

1 Corinthians 16:1–2
Now about the collection for God's people: Do what I told the Galatian churches to do. On the first day of every week, each one of you should set aside a sum of money in keeping with his income, saving it up, so that when I come no collections will have to be made.

Where should I give my tithe?

The Bible teaches us to bring our tithes to the "storehouse." The Old Testament storehouse was the place God designated to keep His abundance and to distribute it to the people. It was also His tabernacle where His name was established. Today, a storehouse is your local church, the place where you receive your spiritual food, nurturing, and fellowship—the place you call home.

God does not need your money in heaven. In heaven there are no unsaved that need to be evangelized. There are no poor who need food. There are no needy who need shelter. No sick people who need health care. No need for counseling facilities or housing for the homeless.

Your tithe should be given to your local church. This is where you are fed, watered, and cared for. If you or a family member becomes ill, it is the local church who will visit you in the hospital, bring meals to your bedside, send flowers and cards of encouragement.

Only the local church can help the elderly with yard work and other special needs. Only the local church can help out with food baskets for the single parent, senior citizen, or the family that has suffered a job loss. It is the local church and its ministries that extend both practical and spiritual food.

Who needs to tithe?

Everyone who is of an age that they understand the purpose, principle, and meaning of the tenth should tithe. The tenth is a measurement of our sacrifice to God. While God does not need our money, He does desire our hearts. James says in 1:17 that every good gift comes from above. God wants to bless us spiritually, financially, and in so many other ways. But He needs our hearts first.

Paying our tithes and giving our offerings are very important principles for Christians to follow. We honor God in our faithfulness in these areas. Our money represents a big part of our heart and our life.

When we honor God in this principle—the principle of setting aside the first tenth—it says to the world that God is first in our lives. It tells God that we belong to Him first and foremost. When we place Him first, not only will our needs be met according to His promises, but an overflow of blessings from heaven to earth will be released on our behalf.

Do I have to tithe? Is tithing voluntary? Is it mandatory for salvation?

While highly recommended, tithing is not a salvation issue. But this is like asking, "Do I have to buy my children Christmas presents?" or, "Do I have to buy flowers for my wife on our anniversary?" or, "Do I have to brush my teeth every day?" or "Do I have to take a bath?" Well, no you don't have to do any of these things, but I do recommend it. Instead of asking the question, "Do I have to tithe?" the issue should be "Thank God that I can tithe, that I can have the blessings of God in my daily life!"

What if I can't afford to tithe?

You can't afford not to tithe. Your difficulty may not be a "earning" problem, but a "spending" problem. When you spend first and give second, your priorities are out of focus. With the right focus, tithing is never a problem. Malachi 3:10 shows us the only way in the Bible for us to test God—we test him with our tithing.

His blessing allows us to decide what to do with 90 percent of our increase; why would you want to be cursed over 10 percent that does not belong to you anyway? I want to live on the 90 percent that is blessed by God. Hebrews 11:16 notes that we cannot please God without faith. When you are walking with Him, it's all about obedience, faith, and trust. You walk in faith, not by your own personal insights.

Faith says to God that your trust in Him is so great that you believe your 90 percent will stretch further with God than 100 percent that you alone are directing. If you think that waiting until you can afford to tithe is right, then you will never feel like you can afford it. If we are all to get through life in good stead, we for sure need the supernatural provision and blessing of God. God is faithful...so give Him a try!

What does money have to do with being a Christian?

Money is a very sensitive issue in our culture even though we are among the most blessed in the world. Often we become very attached to money because of the luxuries in life it brings to us. Yet money is very central to our spiritual experience. Our willingness (or unwillingness) to part with it represents our commitment to Jesus Christ. It is often a measuring stick of our Christian walk. Sometimes we become impatient with our wealth.

When I refer to wealth, I'm referring to having much more than enough. When I say impatient, I mean it in the sense that we always want more. The more we have, the more we want. As we give in to selfishness and lack of discipline when it comes to matters of money, we become bad stewards of all that God has entrusted to our care. Regardless of how we spend our money, it will not be with us forever.

1 Timothy 6:7–10
For we brought nothing into the world, and we can take nothing out of it. But if we have food and clothing, we will be content with that. People who want to get rich fall into temptation and a trap and into many foolish and harmful desires that plunge men into ruin and destruction. For the love

of money is a root of all kinds of evil. Some people, eager for money, have wandered from the faith and pierced themselves with many griefs.

This verse not only reminds us of our temporary use of worldly possessions, but also that we should be content with food and shelter. Many of the world's population do not have enough of either. The verse also tells of the destructive effects upon a person's life resulting from the love of money. It's pretty plain talk. Some people who love money leave the faith and heap grief upon their life.

HEBREWS 13:5
Keep your lives free from the love of money and be content with what you have, because God has said, "Never will I leave you; never will I forsake you."

We are advised and counseled that we should continually examine ourselves to be certain that we are not in love with money. Our motives and decisions must be pure. Money is a means, not an end all. This verse infers that we are not to be focused on gain, but we are to be content because we are in the care of Almighty God. To be discontent is to distrust God's care. To be discontent is to distrust God's power.

Can a person steal from God?

Malachi 3:8 asks the question, "Will a man rob God?" Kind of a thought-provoking question isn't it! In today's language, the question would be: "Are you a thief?" If you are a tither, you may still be just 1 percent short of being a thief. Malachi goes on to say in verse 10, "Bring ye all the tithes into the storehouse." In 1 Corinthians, 16:2, Paul says, "Let every one of you lay by him in store, as God hath prospered him." This was an obvious reference to the tithe.

Tithing and renewal go hand in hand because tithes provide for the release of ministry in the house of God as seen throughout the Old Testament. Nehemiah, seeing the lack of support for the Levites and the house of God forsaken, contended for the tithe in Nehemiah 13:10–12.

Ministry was being prevented because the servants of God had no provision when the people stopped tithing. They were forced to return to their own fields, leaving the house of God without ministers. As affirmed by 1 Corinthians 9:1–11, those being ministered to are to provide for those who are ministering.

God considers giving so important that John 3:16 records, "For God so loved the world, that he gave his only begotten Son, that whosoever believeth in him should not perish, but have everlasting life" (KJV).

My tithing won't amount to much. Why does God need my tithe?

Of course, we know that God does not need any money at all. But He does need our obedience. The widow of Mark 12:41 gave all she had. Whatever we give, either the tenth or beyond the tenth, should be given from the start, off the top, before we commit to anything else. Proverbs 3:9 directs us to honor the Lord from our wealth by giving the first of all our produce: "Honor the LORD with your wealth, with the firstfruits of all your crops."

What if I choose not to tithe?

God has a name for non-tithers. He calls them robbers. He says that they are cursed.

MALACHI 3:8–9
"Will a man rob God? Yet you have robbed Me! But you say, "In what way have we robbed You?" In tithes and offerings. You are cursed with a curse, For you have robbed Me."

What do I get in return for tithing?

Your needs will always be met. God will see to it that you always have shelter, never go hungry and that you will be on the receiving end of the hand of God.

2 CORINTHIANS 9:6–11
"Remember this: Whoever sows sparingly will also reap sparingly, and whoever sows generously will also reap generously.... And God is able to make all grace abound to you, so that in all things at all times, having all that you need, you will abound in every good work. As it is written: "He has scattered abroad his gifts to the poor; his righteousness endures forever." Now he who supplies seed to the sower and bread for food will also supply and increase your store of seed and will enlarge the harvest of your righteousness. You will be made rich in every way so that you can be generous on every occasion, and through us your generosity will result in thanksgiving to God."

Should I tithe on an inheritance?

Yes. An inheritance is an increase. Therefore you must tithe on everything that comes into your possession in that way. When Abraham returned with the spoils of war after the successful defeat of Chedorlaomer and the kings (Genesis 14:17–20), he immediately paid the tithe.

I am self-employed. How should I tithe?

If you work for an hourly wage, you should return a tenth of that to the Lord. If you earn twenty dollars per hour, you must tithe two dollars for every compensated hour. If you are a contractor who builds decks, sheds, buildings, etc., you would tithe on your increase. Your increase would be your gross sale, less your expenses (materials, permits, etc.).

If you are a farmer, you would tithe on proceeds from the sale of the grain, less the cost of the seed, etc. If you are an investor, you would tithe on the sales of your investment (land, house, property, stocks, bonds, etc.), less your initial investment expense.

DEUTERONOMY 14:22
"Thou shalt truly tithe all the increase of thy seed, that the field bringeth forth year by year." (KJV)

Do I tithe on my tax refund?

That depends. If you have been tithing throughout the year on your net, then you certainly must tithe on the monies received from your state and federal return of excess dollars paid. If you have been tithing on your gross income each week (recommended), then it is not necessary to tithe a second time on the same increase. However, monies received via government tax refunds provide an excellent opportunity to give love offerings or special designated offerings to worthy local church projects.

I have a lot of debt...should I tithe?

No doubt, we can give ourselves a variety of excuses why we just cannot tithe and give offerings. It is very easy to rationalize our reasons for disobedience. It is a very simple decision. Are you going to obey His command or disobey?

Should I begin tithing if I cannot meet my present obligations using 100 percent of my income?

It is clear that you have a problem. If it is not due to unavoidable health-care debt or any other unforeseen event, then you certainly need to chat with a nonprofit credit counseling service. Free credit counseling services are available. Your pastor can help you locate one. You may be in financial bondage because of uncontrolled, undisciplined spending habits...often the result of a selfish lifestyle.

If you find yourself overwhelmed with debt, there is not an easy way out. You need practical help and spiritual help. What we sow we reap. Your lifestyle of living beyond your means must cease. But you need to begin to work on the spiritual side of things as well. To tithe with heavy debt does require an act of faith. But faith begins with obedience.

God is very clear on the requirement of tithing and is equally clear in His desire to bless your life. He says that when you tithe, He will rebuke the devourer from your life. In other words, He will keep those losses at bay, financial and otherwise, so that the increase in your life will actually increase in purchasing power. He says to "test" Him and see. God truly is waiting in the wings, wishing you would give it a try. He wants to work a miracle in your financial and spiritual life.

Didn't Jesus say that certain people will always be poor?

Jesus never said that. On the other hand, Christ did say that the poor would always be with us.

MATTHEW 26:11
"For you always have the poor with you." (NASB)

Jesus was not saying that some people will always be poor. He was not saying that some cultures will always be poor. Nor was He saying that the people of some nations will always be poor; He never said "once poor, always poor."

But He was confirming a truth of the world—at any given time there will be poor people. Why is this? Life dictates different seasons for all. All people go through certain times in their life when ill health, lack of employment, unforeseen circumstances, etc., can take away all but the very necessities of life.

There are peaks and valleys in our personal world. Wars come and go. Nations rise and fall. The economies of the nations contract and expand. There are good times and bad times. Life happens. One way to keep struggling without light at the end of your personal financial tunnel is to withhold from God.

2 CORINTHIANS 9:9–11
"As it is written: "He has scattered abroad his gifts to the poor; his righteousness endures forever." Now he who supplies seed to the sower and bread for food will also supply and increase your store of seed and will enlarge the harvest of your righteousness. You will be made rich in every way so that you can be generous on every occasion, and through us your generosity will result in thanksgiving to God."

What is the difference between the "tithe" and giving an "offering"?

The tithe is 10 percent of your increase. According to Deuteronomy, this already belongs to God. It is not yours to spend; it is His alone. An offering is any gift presented to God above the tithe. It is ours to give. Whatever the amount, our offerings are reflections of our gratitude for all that we receive from our heavenly Father. This includes our salvation and spiritual blessings; our family, children, health, shelter, and food; and all of our provision and blessings.

2 CORINTHIANS 9:7
"Each man should give what he has decided in his heart to give, not reluctantly or under compulsion, for God loves a cheerful giver."

Anything outside of the prescribed percentage that already belongs to God represents an offering of love. An offering is not a predetermined percentage. Our offerings become a measure of our love and appreciation for things of the kingdom.

Does God really want to bless me as a result of my tithing?

Certainly! However unless you give the tenth due Him, His blessings cannot be unlocked. Obedience triggers the blessing of God. The widow gave all that she had. Whatever we give, either the tenth or beyond the tenth, should be given from the start, off the top, before we commit to anything else.

In Galatians 6:7, Paul tells us that we should not be deceived by thinking anything other than what we sow we will reap. When we sow disobedience, we reap that harvest. When we sow with our obedience, we reap the many blessings of God.

I have heard that tithing was mandated in the Old Testament under the law, but in the New Testament we are under grace. Is it still true for us today?

Let me refer you to a Scripture found in Matthew: "Do not think that I have come to abolish the Law or the Prophets; I have not come to abolish them but to fulfill them." (5:17)

We can infer that Jesus did not do away with the principle of tithing, but expected it to continue into the future. There are those in the Christian world who inaccurately believe that only the Jewish law required one to tithe and that it cannot be for us today.

But according to Galatians 3:17, the law did not come until 430 years after God instituted tithing through Abraham. And, of course, the law did not invalidate previous covenants ratified by God.

Another example is found in Deuteronomy 5. This listing of the Ten Commandments was good then and is certainly applicable to us today. The tithe was given before the law of Moses and is a theme of our faith, not of the law.

It is not a matter of complying with the law, but a matter of building our faith. When properly entered into, this principle of faith releases our personal financial world from the natural economy of this earth and propels it into God's supernatural economy.

What did Jesus teach concerning tithing?

Jesus Christ endorsed tithing. Jesus Christ did not repeal the law concerning tithing. Instead, He endorsed it. Tithe paying was a general practice during the time of Christ. In the New Testament, the term tithe(s) is found ten times.

The sect that was strictest concerning tithing was the Pharisees. In order to be admitted into the fellowship of the Pharisees, one was obligated to pay his tithe. He was obligated to tithe to the treasury what he bought, what he sold, and what he ate. Jesus commended the Pharisees for tithing in Matthew 23:23. Tithing was about the only thing they were doing right.

Luke 11:42
"But woe to you Pharisees! For you tithe mint and rue and all manner of herbs, and pass by justice and the love of God. These you ought to have done, without leaving the others undone." (NKJV)

Though tithing is not a requirement for salvation, the love of God and the judgment of sin are. The Lord notes that the Pharisees had selective principles that they chose to obey. Jesus said not to leave the tithing undone; rather tithe, and in addition to tithing, recognize the love of God.

In Luke 16:11, Jesus says that if one has not been faithful in the use of his money, how can he expect God to trust him with great riches. He suggests that the principle of obedience is important no matter the amount of sacrifice.

He also said in Matthew 6:20 that we are to lay up for ourselves treasures in heaven, that when we give our tithe and offerings to the work of the Lord, we are investing in souls for the kingdom.

Where else in the New Testament is the "tenth" mentioned?

LUKE 18:12
"'I fast twice a week and give a tenth of all I get.'"

MATTHEW 23:23
"Woe to you, teachers of the law and Pharisees, you hypocrites! You give a tenth of your spices-mint, dill and cummin. But you have neglected the more important matters of the law-justice, mercy and faithfulness. You should have practiced the latter, without neglecting the former."

Jesus was not saying that one should not tithe; He was saying that in addition to all of the outward issues the Pharisees were addressing, they also needed also to be concerned with issues of the heart. Mercy and faith should be practiced along with tithing.

HEBREWS 7:8
"Here mortal men receive tithes, but there he receives them, of whom it is witnessed that he lives." (NKJV)

The New Testament references tithing in the present tense, not the past tense.

1 Corinthians 16:2
"On the first day of every week, each one of you should set aside a sum of money in keeping with his income, saving it up, so that when I come no collections will have to be made."

This New Testament verse and others like it would seem to strongly indicate that the principle of tithing was a common practice. While the specific word tithe is not used here, the presumption is certainly implied. It refers to the first day of the week. It notes that we should lay in store "as God hath prospered" (KJV).

To whom does the tithe belong?

The tithe belongs to God. We "pay," or "return," the tithe. The remaining 90 percent (or 100 percent of what belongs to us) provides us with an opportunity to give offerings. Our "giving" does not start until the tithe has been paid. Our offerings are accepted not by the amount, but by the spirit and attitude in which we give them. The tithe has very little to do with attitude, but has everything to do with obedience.

What should my tithing attitude be?

Perhaps you feel that tithing is just a requirement that must be met. But tithing should be done with joy and peace. It should be an expression of your love. To tithe without joy is to view salvation as a requirement for eternal life, but not to expect any of the blessings God has for His children.

Jesus Christ freely gave His life for your redemption and certainly wants to bless you in very practical ways. Give Him an opportunity to do so!

In the four Gospels, Jesus talks about money issues more than salvation issues. Doesn't this tell you that He knows how greedy and selfish we can be? Surely He knew that we hold on to that which we cannot ultimately keep. Greed comes from selfishness.

Matthew 16:26
"What good will it be for a man if he gains the whole world, yet forfeits his soul? Or what can a man give in exchange for his soul?"

1 Timothy 6:10
For the love of money is a root of all kinds of evil. Some people, eager for money, have wandered from the faith and pierced themselves with many griefs.

It is not about how much money you have; it's about how much money has you. In the end it all comes down to this: The money you spend is gone. The money you keep will someday be gone as you pass from this world to another. The money you give to the Lord is an investment in the kingdom that you take with you when you go.

It's not about how much money you give. It's about your attitude toward money. Don't let your money or possessions become your master. Don't let them dictate your actions and future.

Matthew 6:24
"No one can serve two masters. Either he will hate the one and love the other, or he will be devoted to the one and despise the other. You cannot serve both God and Money."

A bit of advice here—just be faithful in your tithing and giving of offerings. Every day, day in and day out. Be consistent. Be regular. Be timely. Faithfulness is a great virtue in life.

What does obedience have to do with tithing?

Some people "tip," but don't tithe. They give a little here and a little there. There is no consistency to their faithfulness. They eat the seed that God could be using use to get them out of debt, bless their business, and bring favor upon their family.

LEVITICUS 27:30–33
A tithe of everything from the land, whether grain from the soil or fruit from the trees, belongs to the LORD; it is holy to the LORD. If a man redeems any of his tithe, he must add a fifth of the value to it. The entire tithe of the herd and flock—every tenth animal that passes under the shepherd's rod—will be holy to the LORD. He must not pick out the good from the bad or make any substitution. If he does make a substitution, both the animal and its substitute become holy and cannot be redeemed.'

People who do not tithe have forgotten to whom it belongs. They refuse to believe that it is all God's money anyway and all He is asking for is the tenth. If you will give God the tenth, He will make sure that the other 90 percent gets you more in the end. God wants us to bring the firstfruits of our labor to Him. He lets us know what can happen to our money if greed plays a role in our life.

MATTHEW 6:19–21
"Do not store up for yourselves treasures on earth, where moth and rust destroy, and where thieves break in and steal. But store up for yourselves treasures in heaven, where moth and rust do not destroy, and where thieves do not break in and steal. For where your treasure is, there your heart will be also."

MALACHI 3:10–11
"Bring the whole tithe into the storehouse, that there may be food in my house. Test me in this," says the LORD Almighty, "and see if I will not throw open the floodgates of heaven and pour out so much blessing that you will not have room enough for it. I will prevent pests from devouring your crops, and the vines in your fields will not cast their fruit," says the LORD Almighty.

Within the kingdom of God, everything revolves around obedience and choice. You can choose to disobey, ignore the principles of the kingdom, and receive a curse upon your finances—that is to say a plugging up of the conduit of God's blessings upon your finances and life. Alternately you can choose to believe God, be faithful to His Word, act upon His Word through obedience, and be blessed. It is all about attitude and obedience. Do you trust God with your life or not?

God's tithe belongs to your local church. I have met a number of people who adamantly propose that their tithe belongs to whomever they decide to give it. One longtime Christian who faithfully defends the cause of tithing, believes that she is tithing when she gives money to her married children. Of course, there are many people with many needs. Then you have those who somehow drop into your life, whether in person or via the media, who have their hands out.

Help whomever you wish, but don't confuse the tithe with your other charitable giving. The tithe belongs to your local church. This is where you are fed, sustained, and have relationships. Only they will help you should you one day find yourself in need. Only your local church will see to it that you are visited in the hospital or fed when you are without. God's funding plan for the operation of the local church is His tithe, which comes from your increase.

How am I blessed by being obedient?

You are blessed in that God now has the opportunity to unstop the dam that has been holding back His blessing on your life. Obedience triggers the promises of God's Word.

Just remember, Satan desires to steal everything good in your life. But God desires to bless you with every good gift from on high. Many Scriptures support both premises.

John 10:10
"The thief comes only to steal and kill and destroy; I have come that they may have life, and have it to the full."

James 1:17
Every good and perfect gift is from above, coming down from the Father of the heavenly lights, who does not change like shifting shadows.

The "devourer," or Satan, who is your spiritual enemy, would love to steal from you. He would love to steal your financial blessing, your family blessing, your wife and children, and your future from you. By being obedient, not only will God bless you, but He promises to hold Satan away from ruining your life. The bottom line is this:

Until you have given the tenth (the whole tithe) back to God, which He says belongs to Him alone, your giving cannot begin. If you are obedient in your tithing, God will supply all of your needs.

Philippians 4:19
And my God shall supply all your need according to His riches in glory by Christ Jesus. (NKJV)

After obedience in tithing, you can begin giving offerings because your heart is right. Your offerings will bring God's abundance into your life. Malachi 3:10 describes this abundance as overflowing blessings from heaven.

Didn't I earn my money from working hard?

DEUTERONOMY 8:17–18
"You may say to yourself, "My power and the strength of my hands have produced this wealth for me." But remember the LORD your God, for it is he who gives you the ability to produce wealth, and so confirms his covenant, which he swore to your forefathers, as it is today."

Every ability you have comes as a gift from God. Your ability to work, to be healthy, and to enjoy life is nothing short of the grace of God. Your accumulation of material goods, your possessions, your wealth, your blessings all come from God. If you can grasp this little bit of understanding, your entire attitude in life will change.

You must guard against any false attitude or thoughts that you had anything to do with gaining any wealth. That assumption is completely false. Did you work hard as enabled by your Creator? Of course. Were you a diligent laborer? Certainly. But as the Scripture clearly points out, it is Go alone that gives you the ability (strength, wisdom, knowledge, health, etc.) to produce wealth.

Where is the ONLY place in the Bible where we are told to "test" God?

There is only one reference in Scripture where we are told to test God to see if the principle really works. It's like God knows we are skeptical in this area so He throws out an honest challenge to us. He says, "Okay, some of you are already doubting whether or not this really works. So, give it a try…you'll see that I really am true to My Word."

MALACHI 3:10
"Bring the whole tithe into the storehouse, that there may be food in my house. Test me in this," says the LORD Almighty, "and see if I will not throw open the floodgates of heaven and pour out so much blessing that you will not have room enough for it."

How old should my children be before they start tithing?

Parents should teach their children to tithe as soon as they are old enough to understand what giving is all about. They need to understand at an early age the importance of obeying and applying biblical principles.

PROVERBS 22:6
Train a child in the way he should go, and when he is old he will not turn from it.

Do I give 10 percent on my gross income or net income?

Our tithe is always on our increase. You should think even beyond the monetary value of your paycheck. First of all, according to Exodus 23:16, 19, we are to give of our firstfruits. Proverbs 3:9 encourages us to honor the Lord with our wealth and the firstfruits of our crops. Growing up in my father's home, tithing meant our money, our garden, our bonus, our time, etc. Think aggregate, cumulative, the total, the whole, etc.

I am on a fixed income, should I tithe?

It comes down to this: Are you going to trust the promises of God that you will never be in want, or will your trust be only in yourself? Trust God and see how supernatural provision will be yours.

What are the benefits of tithing?

The ministries of the church are funded. The vision of the church is fulfilled. The poor and needy are helped. Since God loves a cheerful giver, we experience the love of God like never before. He blesses our family life both spiritually and financially in ways that could not be experienced before. We experience God's response to our obedience. Tithing triggers the Malachi 3:10–11 test—open heavens and showers of blessings. By stepping out in faith, we enter a whole new realm in the Spirit world. When we walk by faith, we open the door of opportunity to see miracles happen in our life.

What does it mean to "rebuke the devourer"?

MALACHI 3:10–11

Bring ye all the tithes into the storehouse, that there may be meat in mine house, and prove me now herewith, saith the LORD of hosts, if I will not open you the windows of heaven, and pour you out a blessing, that there shall not be room enough to receive it. And I will rebuke the devourer for your sakes, and he shall not destroy the fruits of your ground; neither shall your vine cast her fruit before the time in the field, saith the LORD of hosts. (KJV)

The tithe (the first tenth) does not belong to you. It belongs to God. Many things come against us in our financial life. It may be the loss of a job, auto repair expenses, house maintenance, appliance breakdown, or health-care related expenses. From time to time, we all can acknowledge some difficulty in these areas. And when out-of-nowhere expenses come, they can be burdensome and costly. However, what we don't know is all that God keeps away from us. When we are faithful in our giving, the Word states simply that our crops will be large and that He will keep the insects and plagues away. Whether you are a farmer, a tiller of the ground, or simply planting crops of a nonagricultural nature, you can rest assured that God is working on your behalf.

Should I be giving above my tithe?

Yes. You should give offerings as you become aware of need, to support vision, aid in missions at home and abroad, and give to any other areas that the Holy Spirit prompts you.

LUKE 6:38
"Give, and it will be given to you. A good measure, pressed down, shaken together and running over, will be poured into your lap. For with the measure you use, it will be measured to you."

ACTS 20:35
In everything I did, I showed you that by this kind of hard work we must help the weak, remembering the words the Lord Jesus himself said: "It is more blessed to give than to receive."

It is the very nature of God to give. He gave of Himself. He loves the opportunity to give gifts to His children. When we give, gifts are given to us. Giving is often the result of our ability and desire to respond to specific needs. Sometimes giving is an act of faith on our part. When we move into faith giving, it is the very nature of God to respond in much the same way.

I pay my tithes regularly, with consistency and accuracy. But how many and how much should I give in offerings?

2 CORINTHIANS 9:6
Remember this: Whoever sows sparingly will also reap sparingly, and whoever sows generously will also reap generously.

Chapter 5

The Cycle of Giving

$\mathscr{T}$he Scripture has this to say about the cycle of nature. "All streams flow into the sea, yet the sea is never full. To the place the streams come from, there they return again" (Ecclesiastes 1:7 NIV).

There is a cycle to the elements in nature as seen in God's great creation. Take a seed, for example. It is hidden away, ever so small, just waiting there beneath the sod of the earth. But at the appropriate time—when the earth begins to warm, the rain begins to fall and the sun begins to shine—the seed begins to grow roots.

As the earth fertilizes the roots, a bud begins to form and peak out on the surface of the earth. In time, the plant grows to full blossom. Eventually it releases a fragrance, which attracts pollinators, bees and bugs. When the plant matures, it drops new seeds upon the ground. The seed, in turn, waits just below the surface until a new season begins.

Water is another example of recycling. Water constantly renews its purity by cycling itself from a liquid (or a solid) into a vapor and back again. The change to a vapor removes most impurities and allows water to return to Earth in its clean form.

The study of water or hydrology starts with the water cycle, the process by which water renews itself. Since the cycle is continuous, it doesn't really have a beginning, but a convenient place to start studying it is with precipitation (rain, snow, sleet and hail). When precipitation falls to earth, several things can happen. It can be absorbed into the soil. According to the United States Environmental Protection Agency, this is called infiltration. This process allows water to seep into the earth and be stored underground as groundwater.

Precipitation can also become runoff, flowing into rivers and streams. Water can evaporate or it can be returned to the atmosphere by transpiration through plants. Precipitation can also be stored. An ice cap is a form of storage.

In temperate climates, water is found in depression storage or surface water puddles, ditches and anywhere else that runoff water can gather. This is a temporary form of storage. Water will evaporate from the surface and infiltrate into the ground. It will be absorbed by plants and transpired back into the air. It will flow to other areas. This cycling of water is continuous.

Money can only affect our world around us for the gospel if it is put into circulation. The Dead Sea is dead because it only takes in and gives nothing out. The law of living is giving. If money is to be useful, it must be used. When increase comes our way, we should use it, not only for our needs, but also for the good of others.

Treasures on earth can become paths to building heavenly treasures if they are used and distributed for the glory of God. Jesus understood clearly that, in the consumer culture of this world, we live in a constant battleground for our affections, our heart and our soul.

There is also a cycle to money and its use. Money can be similarly compared to the cycle of water in nature. Did you know that money is only profitable when it is used? If we are to live life abundantly as Christians, we must follow the scriptural principle of giving. Our measure of giving determines the measure of how we will receive.

Luke 6:38 states, "Give, and it shall be given unto you; good measure, pressed down, and shaken together, and running over, shall men give into your bosom. For with the same measure that ye mete withal it shall be measured to you again." (KJV) The more you give, the more He gives back to you. He gives back to the giver. Giving is for your sake, because God gives to givers.

Does the receiver benefit? Yes, in the sense that needs are met. But it is the giver who benefits the most. In II Corinthians 9:6-15, Paul gives clear instructions to the church concerning giving. Verse 7 notes that God will love the giver in a special way. Verse 8 says God will provide for him. Verses 9-11 speak of his resources being multiplied and enriched. God sees to it that givers are receivers. They obtain money, prosperity, blessing and eternal rewards. And they grow in faith.

Giving money is so significant to God because giving money is a way to give of yourself. Matthew 6:19-21 reminds us, "Lay not up for yourselves treasures upon earth, where moth and rust doth corrupt, and where thieves break through and steal: But lay up for yourselves treasures in heaven, where neither moth nor rust doth corrupt, and where thieves do not break through nor steal: For where your treasure is, there will your heart be also" (KJV).

Giving money is significant to God because giving money is a way to give of yourself.

In Bible times, riches often consisted of beautiful clothing and precious metals. Immense value resided in garments passed down from generation to generation. Jacob gave Joseph a coat of many colors. Joseph gave Benjamin five changes of clothing. Samson promised thirty changes of garments to the one who guessed his riddle. It was very common to place a great deal of importance in clothing. There was a cycle to the flow of wealth.

In the days of the ancient past, people of influence had treasures that consisted of fine clothing, gold, silver, gems, wine, lands, etc. Any of this in abundance was considered of great value and wealth. Today, we are still thrilled with possessions of jewelry, fine cars, boats, clothing, electronic equipment, houses, money and so on. While Jesus said that the poor would always be with us, He also made clear the obligation of the wealthy to the needy. In ancient times, there were many examples of brotherhood. Joseph gave his brothers changes of garments. Achan apparently coveted a beautiful Babylonian garment. Today, there are many food drives to feed the hungry and many clothing drives to provide warm apparel for the needy.

James said to the rich men who had hoarded up clothing and wealth, "Your riches are corrupted, and your garments are moth-eaten" (James 5:2 NKJV). In other words, your unused wealth will get you nowhere. The problem here was unused money. These men had gathered riches for riches sake. James said, "The rust of them (your wealth) shall be a witness against you" (James 5:3 KJV). Rust is a symbol of disuse. It is a sign of inactivity.

Of course, we know that rust can destroy even the best of tools and moths also attack things that we consume. Literally, rust in its destructive path will eat into and destroy nearly everything. Rust will eventually corrode all metal including silver and gold. Figuratively speaking, rust can be anything that would destroy you and your life. In short, all of your treasures, whether physical or otherwise, can be destroyed.

The treasures of the kingdom, however, are eternal. When we concentrate on using our earthly possessions to bring glory to God, then we are storing up treasures in heaven.

Chapter 6

8 Principles of Sowing & Reaping

$\mathcal{S}$ome events seem to be a way of life. For example, you never get a busy signal when you dial a wrong number. Children never seem to spill their food on dirty floors and the line at the grocery store is always the longest when you are in a hurry.

It seems that while waiting in line at the bank, the gas station, or the grocery store, the other line next to you moves faster. I was in a local variety store in Portland, Oregon, by the name of Fred Meyer. While headed for the 10-items-or-less line, an entire family cut just in front of me. I was in a hurry, but waited until they all crowded into the line in front of me. Their cart was filled with grocery items. As I watched in surprise, the parents passed out the money and proceeded to divide up the cart between themselves and the kids!

The law of living is giving.
If money is to be useful, it must be used.

Additional laws might include: it always rains on the weekends, you seem to get sick on your day off, etc. Perhaps they could be called Murphy's Other Laws. Some of these laws you can live without knowing about. However, there are some laws you ignore at your own risk of potential destruction.

There are basic laws of nature. In regards to sowing and reaping, here are some things to consider.

1.
The seed we plant is the same kind of seed we reap...seed of its kind.

One phenomenon of God's creation is that the seed we plant is from the fruit which was harvested. We see this in life. Parents often see in their children the characteristics of themselves, both good and bad. Each of us must set good examples, for life is spent planting. You have no choice but to sow. When we sow financial seeds into God's kingdom, we benefit from the same.

2.
We determine the size of the harvest at the time of planting (II Corinthians 9:6,8,11).

The farmer who plants hundreds or thousands of acres knows that, barring some natural disaster, he is going to reap more than he planted, but always in proportion to what he planted. One who is generous with his time, talents and resources is going to reap generously. One who is generous with love, appreciation and mercy will reap in the proportion that he sows those things.

The man who gives beyond his tithe (the tithe belongs to the Lord) has just begun to give. The more one gives, the more one reaps. But don't just look for repayment in monetary measure. Good health is more important than money. A family serving the Lord is more important than dollars.

3.
We will always have a harvest (Malachi 3:10; Galatians 6:9).

When you sow, you will always reap! This law is as sure as the rising and going down of the sun. The success of this harvest is not determined by natural laws, but the success is governed by the Lord Himself. Should you sow your seed into your local place of worship from which you and your family receive much benefit? Of course! Will you reap the harvest? Certainly! You and your family reap a good harvest every time your local pastor preaches the Word and sows good seed into your lives.

4.
You will usually reap later than you sow.

In the American Midwest, farms are everywhere. You don't have to be around a farm too long to learn that both growth and decay take time. The same is true in our spiritual lives.

Perhaps this is the reason Paul warned that we shouldn't be deceived. There's a caution in sowing to the flesh. Nothing seems to happen right away. Marriages do not collapse in an instant. People become deceived and don't realize what's happening until they are trapped.

While we receive much immediate benefit when we sow into our local church, it doesn't stop there. We continue to reap the harvest throughout our lives, because the seed continues to multiply.

5.
We will always reap more than we planted (Matthew 13:8).

When we plant a kernel of corn, we reap a stalk with several ears of corn on it. On the ears of corn are hundreds of kernels of corn. So it is with a blade of wheat. Only God could design such a wonder. The law of increased return is what makes farming a workable business enterprise. But sowing to the Spirit results in eternal life. The NIV translates I Corinthians 2:9, "No eye has seen, no ear has heard, no mind conceived, what God has prepared for those who love him."

6.
There is a season for planting and a season for harvesting (Ecclesiastes 3:1, 2).

Not all harvesting follows immediately. The time element is important. If the seed germinates before its proper time, a harvest can be lost. Many give as if there will not be a harvest. Some people think God has not noted what they are planting, simply because they have not experienced a harvest. But if we plant the seed, a harvest will come. For example, consider Proverbs 22:6 from the NIV: "Train a child in the way he should go, and when he is old he will not turn from it." The promise is, if we continue to plant the seed of godly training when the child is young, then in a different season of life the child will not forget their training. Thus, as parents or grandparents, we enjoy the harvest, even though it might be years later.

7.
Seed can be sown secretly; however, the harvest is always viewed by many.

We do not see all the work, sweat and tears that a person has expended to plant the seed. It may seem to those who were not involved in the labor that the seed was just planted yesterday. When we see the lives of people who are reaping a great harvest of blessing, we should remember that it sometimes took years of faithful cultivating and sowing to bring them to the place where they are today. The harvest they are now reaping, visible and apparent to all, required hours of sacrifice, pain, and toil when nobody else was watching.

8.
We are responsible to sow and God is responsible for the harvest.

We are laborers together with God. God does not produce failures; He is the Lord of the harvest. With these laws God has set in order, we need to sow seed that is going to bring fruit both now and for eternity. He is the Lord of the harvest. As we enter each new season, we must start by planting.

Chapter 7

4 Secrets of The Seed

$\mathscr{H}$ere are four key principles that relate to seed sowing and your personal finances:

1. God Owns the Seed

When you understand this first principle, you will be in a right position to prosper; you will be able to then make God your partner. Prospering by partnering with God is first done by accepting this fact: God owns everything! You do not own anything.

You may have a business that you operate or manage, but you are only doing what God has allowed you to do. Christians don't own anything at all; they merely manage things for God. When you die, how much of your money will you leave behind? All of it! When you die, how much of your money will you take with you? None of it!

Ultimately, you don't own anything. You won't take your house with you. You won't take your land with you. You won't take any of the wealth or possessions with you that you have managed to accumulate here on earth. You won't even take your body because you don't even own it. When your spirit leaves your body, it will turn to dust. You may currently possess certain things, but mere possession is not ownership. Those things that you possess can be taken from you in an instant.

> PSALM 24:1 (NIV)
> *"The earth is the LORD's, and everything in it, the world, and all who live in it"*

> HAGGAI 2:8 (NIV)
> *"'The silver is mine and the gold is mine,' declares the LORD Almighty"*

> PSALM 50:10,11 (NIV)
> *"For every animal of the forest is mine, and the cattle on a thousand hills. I know every bird in the mountains, and the creatures of the field are mine"*

You can possess, but it is God who owns. You may earn a living, but it is God who gives you the ability to earn. How does this relate to the laws of sowing and reaping? If God is the true owner of your possessions, then your role is that of a steward. With the resources God has entrusted to you, you must seek to sow into his kingdom in order to reap a heavenly harvest.

What does this look like in everyday life? Sowing into God's kingdom means setting aside a portion of your paycheck to give into the lives of others, instead of just thinking about your own needs. It means listening and giving with compassion as missionaries describe the needs around the world. Sowing into God's kingdom means daily looking to God and asking Him, "How do you want me to spend Your money today?"

2. You are a Steward of the Seed

The principles upon which a person builds his financial future are very important. They can ensure security in the later years of a person's life. The manner in which finances are acquired and disbursed must be based on sound moral guidelines. The desire for money can become an obsession. When it does, nothing can satisfy. Peace of mind is gone. The joy of a new day gives way to worry about retaining what one has and gaining more and more.

Our life's stewardship should reflect God's interest in all that He has entrusted us with. Genesis 1:26 records that God made man to rule over all the earth and all life on earth, both plant and animal. In Genesis 2:15, man was made steward over the Garden in which there was gold, precious stones and rivers.

In other words, man was created for more than going to heaven after a lifetime of waiting. He was created to be a faithful steward over the work of God's hands. This is a lot of trust that God places in our lives. It is more than just finances. It is our entire life and how we handle it with faithfulness, responsibility, accountability, honesty and integrity. Stewardship is bringing everything we have to offer to the Lordship of Christ. What kind of a person makes a good steward? A person who has a great respect for God and his creation.

Money and possessions, at best, only last a lifetime. At worst, they don't last at all. They are but a fleeting vapor, just like our lives. Why spend all of your life trying to accumulate something that will never last? How much better it would be for you to spend your time investing in things that are of eternal nature.

Some of the most miserable people in the world are people who literally have everything. Everything, that is, except a loving family and a clean heart! Everything except honor. Everything except the blessing of God. The Lord has better things to come for those who have been good stewards of all He has entrusted to them.

Money and possessions, at best, only last a lifetime. At worst, they don't last at all.

Leaving all scruples and morals for the sake of money is a foolish thing to do. Yet that is just what many men and women are doing today. And their seemingly apparent success sometimes causes an infectious greed that hangs upon people who should know better. Some people don't seek to put in an honest day's work for an honest dollar, a day's work for a day's pay. They get caught up in the spirit of the fast buck. Easy money; unearned income; get rich quick!

God is concerned about our actions and motives. What we are is far more important than what we possess! The person who takes stewardship seriously handles life, talents, strength and money as a trust from God.

3. Be Careful Not to Hoard the Seed

It is important to continually invest the seed that God has given to you. This doesn't mean putting your entire paycheck in the offering basket at church! It does, however, mean that you should guard yourself from an attitude that hoards the seed God gives you.

There is nothing wrong or evil about money itself. It is just a medium of exchange for goods or services rendered. However, there is often something wrong with our attitude toward money. We always seem to want more than we have.

This dissatisfaction with our current state or condition can be blamed on our Adamic human nature. Discontentment and coveting what belongs to another can cause problems with money. Paul wrote in I Timothy 6:9, "But they that will be rich fall into temptation and a snare, and into many foolish and hurtful lusts..." (KJV)

Many people who have lived for money and success have failed God. When a person's attitude is not right toward money, he or she may fall into the trap of materialism. If, on the other hand, we use the monetary blessings God has given us to finance His cause and further His kingdom, we will be blessed accordingly. I Timothy 6:7 reminds us, "For we brought nothing into this world, and it is certain we can carry nothing out." (KJV)

Acts 17:28 (KJV)
"For in him we live and move and have our being"

DEUTERONOMY **8:18 (NIV)**
"But remember the LORD your God, for it is He who gives you the ability to produce wealth..."

EZEKIEL **18:4 (NIV)**
"For every living soul belongs to me"

ROMANS **12:1 (NIV)**
"Therefore, I urge you, brothers, in view of God's mercy, to offer your bodies as living sacrifices, holy and pleasing to God"

PSALM **100:3 (NIV)**
"Know that the LORD is God. It is he who made us, and we are his; we are his people, the sheep of his pasture"

I CORINTHIANS **6:19-20 (NIV)**
"You are not your own; you were bought at a price. Therefore honor God with your body"

Because we are not our own, we should dedicate to God all that we are, all that we own and all that we will ever be. You are God's, so all you have belongs to God. You simply manage your possessions for Him. Your business belongs to God.

When everything you have belongs to God, it takes all of the pressure off you. For example, let's say you are a farmer and your farm belongs to God. If the weather is dry and it doesn't rain, you don't have to worry about it because it belongs to God. If your business is dedicated to God, it becomes His problem and not yours. In business, when you partner with God, He not only will bless it, He will let you enjoy prosperity also.

But there is a caution not to keep everything for yourself. Instead of trying to figure out how little we can give to God, try giving it all to Him and ask Him how much you should keep.

4. Enjoy some of the seed!

The apostle Paul realized that, although everything in the universe belongs to God, if we partner with Him, He allows us to keep some of everything He provides. The farmer who harvests the crop has a right to eat some of it. The one who plants the vineyard gets to enjoy some of its fruit.

Luke 6:38 (KJV)
"Give, and it shall be given unto you"

Chapter 8

Praying for The Practical

$\mathcal{T}$ithing is a priority of giving our first fruits. But others areas of our lives also need adjustment from time to time. Do you make time to pray the truths of God's Word over the practical use of your finances? Nehemiah was a man who understood the power of combining specific prayer with the practical details of his life.

When he first received the report that the walls of Jerusalem had been torn down and destroyed by fire, his first reaction was to turn to God in prayer and fasting (Neh. 1:3-4). When he was later asked by the king about what he would need to rebuild the walls, we read that he first offered up a prayer to God and then asked the king for the specific materials he would need (Neh. 2: 4, 7-8).

Then, when facing heavy opposition during the building project, we read that he responded in two ways. After first crying out to God in prayer (Neh. 4:4, 9), he then placed guards behind the lowest parts of the wall in the most vulnerable places (Neh. 4:13). Nehemiah's mentality for moving forward in his God-given project combined prayer with the practical.

God's Word contains powerful truths which relate to different areas of your finances, including savings, borrowing, investing, and budgeting. Most of us have a deep desire to apply the truths of God's Word into our lives. Even if we don't have a huge project in front of us, as Nehemiah did, we have a longing to walk in financial success, wisdom, and freedom.

The Power of Focused Prayer

Desiring financial breakthrough, however, is often a far-cry from reality. When Monday morning rolls around, the kids are still asking for new clothes, the car needs to be fixed, and the bills need to be paid. Imagine that your current financial situation is like a wall that is being built.

Remember that, in Nehemiah's situation, he placed guards behind the most vulnerable places in order to ward off the attacks of the enemy. Do you see any weak, vulnerable areas in your "financial wall" that are prone to attack?

How can you make sure that you are moving forward in your financial vision, protected from everyday hindrances? We believe that you need a "Nehemiah mentality" that combines specific prayer with the everyday details of your life.

The financial prayer guide following is intended to help you pray over 14 specific areas of your finances (derived from key chapters in this book). While some prayer guides are intended to be prayed in full each day, I would suggest a more simple approach for this one, offering up a prayer for your finances in the morning and in the evening. It is my hope that, through adopting a Nehemiah mentality, you can move forward in the financial vision that God has for you!

Weekly Financial Prayer Guide

SUNDAY

Giving

Lord, I thank you for giving the ultimate Gift to me, your Son (John 3:16). *Please help me today to be conscious of giving opportunities* (II Cor. 8:12-15, Col. 4:3-5), *obedient in my tithing* (Mal. 3:10), *and compassionate for those who are in need* (Prov. 19:17).

Wise-decisions

Lord, you are so faithful to give wisdom to me when I ask you for it (James 1:5)! *In my decision-making this week, I ask you for the courage to step out* (Josh. 1:9), *the discernment to weigh the costs involved* (II Cor. 9:7, Lk. 14:28), *and the commitment to finish what I have started* (Col. 4:17, II Cor. 8:11).

MONDAY

Seeking the Kingdom

Lord, today I acknowledge your command to seek first your kingdom and your righteousness (Matt. 6:33). *Help me to avoid the lust for greed and money* (I Tim. 6:6-11), *to be* content with what I have (Heb. 13:5), and to live for eternal things (Phil. 3:19-20).

Sowing

Lord, thank you that you have called me to sow cheerfully and generously, expecting a harvest in time (II Cor. 9:6-15). Help me not to grow weary in well-doing (Gal. 6:9), sowing to please the Spirit (Gal. 6:8) with my words (Eph. 4:29), with my time (I Chron. 12:32), and with my money (II Cor. 9:6-15).

TUESDAY

Stewardship

Lord, I am amazed that you have entrusted me with talents and resources that you want me to multiply (Matt. 25:14-30)! I ask you today for help in being diligent with my time (Ps. 90:12), faithful with my responsibilities (Col. 3:23), and both wise and gracious in my communication with others (Col. 4:6, Prov. 22:11).

Self-discipline

Lord, I need your help to be self-disciplined so that, like an athlete in training, I can win the prize (I Cor. 9:24-27)! Help me to know the short-term and long-term financial goals I need to work on (Col. 1:9-10, Phil. 3:13-14). Please grant me the grace to both resist distractions (Prov. 4:25-26, Ecc. 10:16-17) and take time for creative rest (Ps. 23:2-3).

WEDNESDAY

Persevering

I thank you, Jesus, that when troubles come my way, it is an opportunity for joy (James 1:2)! In any financial challenges I am facing, I ask you for help to discern the root *of the problems* (I Tim. 6:10) *while praising you in the midst of them* (Job 1:21-22, Ps. 27:5-6). *Though life is busy, help me to invest in focused prayers* (Phil. 4:6) *that will give birth to peace* (Phil. 4:7), *new direction* (Acts 13:2-3), *and eventual solutions* (II Chron. 20:13-24).

Vision

I give you praise, Lord, that you've called me to reach forward unto those things that are before me (Phil. 3:13-14). *Grant me great wisdom to lay hold of renewed financial vision for my life* (Col. 1:9-10, Neh. 1:4, 2:4-8), *resisting the procrastination* (Prov. 6:6-11) *and distractions* (Gal. 5:7-9) *that would stand in my way.*

THURSDAY

Planning

Lord, thank you that, by the hand of your Spirit, I am able to make wise plans in how to invest my money, time, and resources (Matt. 25:14-30, I Chron 29:3-5 Zech. 4:6). *Help me to be wise in my budgeting and to close the doors on unnecessary spending* (Prov. 21:20). *Enable me to set aside the time to seek out good counsel* (Prov. 15:22), *making plans that are wise, just, and ordered of You* (Prov. 12:5, Jms. 4:15-16).

Savings

Thanks, Lord, for the simple example of the ants who know how to wisely store up for the future (Prov. 6:8). *Help me not to spend everything I make* (Prov. 21:20), *but to wisely discern the amount I need to set aside for future needs, emergencies, commitments, and long-range goals* (II. Cor. 8:10-11, Prov. 6:8, 31:21, 27).

FRIDAY

Debt-free

Lord, your ways are higher (Is. 55:8-9)! *I ask you to renew my mind with your divine perspective about debt, credit, and borrowing* (Prov. 11:15, 22:7, Rom. 13:6-8). *Help me to be intentional about paying off my debts* (Rom. 13:6-8), *and let me be faithful in the little things of life so that you can entrust me with more* (Lk. 16:10-12, 19:18-19).

Wise-Lifestyle

Thank you, Lord, that you have called me to be a person who is careful and wise (Eph. 5:15). *In the way that I live, help me to be resourceful and yet generous* (Prov. 21:20, Prov. 11:25), *led by your Spirit in both the little choices I make and in my major decisions* (Lk. 16:10-12, Jms. 4:15). *Let me be known as a person who is full of the Spirit and wisdom* (Acts 6:3).

SATURDAY

Watchman

Lord, you have called me to diligently guard the vulnerable areas of my life that are prone to attack (Prov. 4:20-27, Neh. 4:13, I Pet. 3:11). *Help me to avoid get-rich schemes* (I Tim. 6:9), *unwise investments* (Lk 14:28-30), *hasty purchases* (Prov. 14:8), *and any deceptions of others* (Prov. 9:13-18) *that would cause me to stumble and fall. Make me a diligent watchman* (Neh. 4:13, Ezek. 22:30) *who knows the enemy's schemes in advance* (II Cor. 2:11, II Kgs. 6:10), *guarding and protecting that which you've entrusted to me.*

Investing

Lord, thank you that you've called me to live a life of multiplication and not mere addition (Matt. 13:23, 25:14-30). *As I look to you for vision for the future, help me to consider my options for investing* (Prov. 21:5, 31:16-24), *discerning the proper times* (Ps. 90:12, I Chron. 12:32, Ecc. 8:5-6) *and sowing with wisdom* (Lk 19:13-26).

Chapter 9

Generosity & Liberality in the Bible

Generosity

1 KINGS 10:13
And King Solomon gave the queen of Sheba all she desired, whatever she asked, besides what Solomon had given her according to the royal generosity. So she turned and went to her own country, she and her servants.

ESTHER 1:7
And they served drinks in golden vessels, each vessel being different from the other, with royal wine in abundance, according to the generosity of the king.

ESTHER 2:18
Then the king made a great feast, the Feast of Esther, for all his officials and servants; and he proclaimed a holiday in the provinces and gave gifts according to the generosity of a king.

Isaiah 32:8
But a generous man devises generous things, And by generosity he shall stand.

2 Corinthians 8:2-7
Out of the most severe trial, their overflowing joy and their extreme poverty welled up in rich generosity. For I testify that they gave as much as they were able, and even beyond their ability. Entirely on their own, they urgently pleaded with us for the privilege of sharing in this service to the saints. And they did not do as we expected, but they gave themselves first to the Lord and then to us in keeping with God's will. So we urged Titus, since he had earlier made a beginning, to bring also to completion this act of grace on your part. But just as you excel in everything-in faith, in speech, in knowledge, in complete earnestness and in your love for us-see that you also excel in this grace of giving.

2 Corinthians 9:5
Therefore I thought it necessary to exhort the brethren to go to you ahead of time, and prepare your generous gift beforehand, which you had previously promised, that it may be ready as a matter of generosity and not as a grudging obligation.

2 Corinthians 9:10-14
Now he who supplies seed to the sower and bread for food will also supply and increase your store of seed and will enlarge the harvest of your righteousness. You will be made rich in every way so that you can be generous on every occasion, and through us your generosity will result in thanksgiving to God. This service that you perform is not only supplying the needs of God's people but is also overflowing in many expressions of thanks to God. Because of the service by which you have proved yourselves, men will praise God for the obedience that accompanies your confession of the gospel of Christ, and for your generosity in sharing with them and with everyone else.

2 Corinthians 8:2-7
Out of the most severe trial, their overflowing joy and their extreme poverty welled up in rich generosity. For I testify that they gave as much as they were able, and even beyond their ability. Entirely on their own, they urgently pleaded with us for the privilege of sharing in this service to the saints. And they did not do as we expected, but they gave themselves first to the Lord and then to us in keeping with God's will. So we urged Titus,

94

since he had earlier made a beginning, to bring also to completion this act of grace on your part. But just as you excel in everything-in faith, in speech, in knowledge, in complete earnestness and in your love for us-see that you also excel in this grace of giving.

2 CORINTHIANS 9:10-14

Now he who supplies seed to the sower and bread for food will also supply and increase your store of seed and will enlarge the harvest of your righteousness. You will be made rich in every way so that you can be generous on every occasion, and through us your generosity will result in thanksgiving to God. This service that you perform is not only supplying the needs of God's people but is also overflowing in many expressions of thanks to God. Because of the service by which you have proved yourselves, men will praise God for the obedience that accompanies your confession of the gospel of Christ, and for your generosity in sharing with them and with everyone else.

Liberality

ROMANS 12:6-8

Having then gifts differing according to the grace that is given to us, let us use them: if prophecy, let us prophesy in proportion to our faith; or ministry, let us use it in our ministering; he who teaches, in teaching; he who exhorts, in exhortation; he who gives, with liberality; he who leads, with diligence; he who shows mercy, with cheerfulness.

2 CORINTHIANS 8:1-2

Moreover, brethren, we make known to you the grace of God bestowed on the churches of Macedonia: that in a great trial of affliction the abundance of their joy and their deep poverty abounded in the riches of their liberality.

2 CORINTHIANS 9:10-11

Now may He who supplies seed to the sower, and bread for food, supply and multiply the seed you have sown and increase the fruits of your righteousness, while you are enriched in everything for all liberality, which causes thanksgiving through us to God.

Chapter 10

Tithing In Scripture

GENESIS 14:18–20
Then Melchizedek king of Salem brought out bread and wine; he was the priest of God Most High. And he blessed him and said: "Blessed be Abram of God Most High, Possessor of heaven and earth; And blessed be God Most High, Who has delivered your enemies into your hand." And he gave him a tithe of all.

LEVITICUS 27:30
And all the tithe of the land, whether of the seed of the land or of the fruit of the tree, is the LORD's. It is holy to the LORD.

LEVITICUS 27:31
If a man wants at all to redeem any of his tithes, he shall add one-fifth to it.

LEVITICUS 27:32
And concerning the tithe of the herd or the flock, of whatever passes under the rod, the tenth one shall be holy to the LORD.

NUMBERS 18:21

Behold, I have given the children of Levi all the tithes in Israel as an inheritance in return for the work which they perform, the work of the tabernacle of meeting.

NUMBERS 18:24

For the tithes of the children of Israel, which they offer up as a heave offering to the LORD, I have given to the Levites as an inheritance; therefore I have said to them, "Among the children of Israel they shall have no inheritance."

NUMBERS 18:25–27

Then the LORD spoke to Moses, saying, "Speak thus to the Levites, and say to them: 'When you take from the children of Israel the tithes which I have given you from them as your inheritance, then you shall offer up a heave offering of it to the LORD, a tenth of the tithe.'"

NUMBERS 18:26

Speak thus to the Levites, and say to them: "When you take from the children of Israel the tithes which I have given you from them as your inheritance, then you shall offer up a heave offering of it to the LORD, a tenth of the tithe."

NUMBERS 18:28

Thus you shall also offer a heave offering to the LORD from all your tithes which you receive from the children of Israel, and you shall give the LORD's heave offering from it to Aaron the priest.

DEUTERONOMY 12:6

There you shall take your burnt offerings, your sacrifices, your tithes, the heave offerings of your hand, your vowed offerings, your freewill offerings, and the firstborn of your herds and flocks.

DEUTERONOMY 12:11

Then there will be the place where the LORD your God chooses to make His name abide. There you shall bring all that I command you: your burnt offerings, your sacrifices, your tithes, the heave offerings of your hand, and all your choice offerings which you vow to the LORD.

DEUTERONOMY 12:17
You may not eat within your gates the tithe of your grain or your new wine or your oil, of the firstlings of your herd or your flock, of any of your offerings which you vow, of your freewill offerings, or of the heave offering of your hand.

DEUTERONOMY 14:22
You shall truly tithe all the increase of your grain that the field produces year by year.

DEUTERONOMY 14:23
And you shall eat before the LORD your God, in the place where He chooses to make His name abide, the tithe of your grain and your new wine and your oil, of the firstborn of your herds and your flocks, that you may learn to fear the LORD your God always.

DEUTERONOMY 14:28
At the end of every third year you shall bring out the tithe of your produce of that year and store it up within your gates.

DEUTERONOMY 26:12
When you have finished laying aside all the tithe of your increase in the third year—the year of tithing—and have given it to the Levite, the stranger, the fatherless, and the widow, so that they may eat within your gates and be filled,

2 CHRONICLES 31:5
As soon as the commandment was circulated, the children of Israel brought in abundance the firstfruits of grain and wine, oil and honey, and of all the produce of the field; and they brought in abundantly the tithe of everything.

2 CHRONICLES 31:12
Then they faithfully brought in the offerings, the tithes, and the dedicated things; Cononiah the Levite had charge of them, and Shimei his brother was the next.

Nehemiah 10:37
To bring the firstfruits of our dough, our offerings, the fruit from all kinds of trees, the new wine and oil, to the priests, to the storerooms of the house of our God; and to bring the tithes of our land to the Levites, for the Levites should receive the tithes in all our farming communities.

Nehemiah 10:38
And the priest, the descendant of Aaron, shall be with the Levites when the Levites receive tithes; and the Levites shall bring up a tenth of the tithes to the house of our God, to the rooms of the storehouse.

Nehemiah 12:44
And at the same time some were appointed over the rooms of the storehouse for the offerings, the firstfruits, and the tithes, to gather into them from the fields of the cities the portions specified by the Law for the priests and Levites; for Judah rejoiced over the priests and Levites who ministered.

Nehemiah 13:12
Then all Judah brought the tithe of the grain and the new wine and the oil to the storehouse.

Nehemiah 13:5
And he had prepared for him a large room, where previously they had stored the grain offerings, the frankincense, the articles, the tithes of grain, the new wine and oil, which were commanded to be given to the Levites and singers and gatekeepers, and the offerings for the priests.

Amos 4:4
Come to Bethel and transgress, at Gilgal multiply transgression; bring your sacrifices every morning, your tithes every three days.

Malachi 3:8
Will a man rob God? Yet you have robbed Me! But you say, "In what way have we robbed You?" In tithes and offerings.

Malachi 3:10
"Bring all the tithes into the storehouse, that there may be food in My house, and try Me now in this," says the LORD of hosts, "If I will not open for you the windows of heaven and pour out for you such blessing that there will not be room enough to receive it."

Matthew 23:23
"Woe to you, scribes and Pharisees, hypocrites! For you pay tithe of mint and anise and cummin, and have neglected the weightier matters of the law: justice and mercy and faith. These you ought to have done, without leaving the others undone."

Luke 11:42
"But woe to you Pharisees! For you tithe mint and rue and all manner of herbs, and pass by justice and the love of God. These you ought to have done, without leaving the others undone."

Luke 18:12
"I fast twice a week; I give tithes of all that I possess."

Hebrews 7:5
And indeed those who are of the sons of Levi, who receive the priesthood, have a commandment to receive tithes from the people according to the law, that is, from their brethren, though they have come from the loins of Abraham;

Hebrews 7:6
But he whose genealogy is not derived from them received tithes from Abraham and blessed him who had the promises.

Hebrews 7:8
Here mortal men receive tithes, but there he receives them, of whom it is witnessed that he lives.

Hebrews 7:9
Even Levi, who receives tithes, paid tithes through Abraham, so to speak.

Summary

$\mathcal{S}$o many people today are on a quest to accumulate possessions and wealth. It is hard for all of us to be content with what we have when the world's entire system is geared toward making us unhappy with everything we have and desirous of everything we don't have. From advertising to attitude, we face a discontented culture.

How much money do we want to be content? Usually just a little bit more. Money cannot buy contentment or happiness. It is very hard for us to be satisfied with what we do have, but we need to strive for contentment and contend for happiness.

There is certainly nothing wrong with making money, so long as making money does not violate the laws of our land and the principles of God's Word. The all-for-me and none-for-others way of man's thinking is immoral.

The person of principle who subscribes to the values of the Bible will be a good steward who obeys the law of giving by faithfully tithing. This person will find happiness in exact proportion to the degree that he gives. He will be content with his life and all that it affords.

The story of Matthew 19 is the history of one who was a great young man; a good man; and it seems a principled man. He belonged to the ruling class of his time in history. But even in his culture, he was apparently influenced by a society of peers involved in hoarding finances.

Because the quantity of his possessions and personal wealth was substantial, he made a choice to hang on to what he had. Instead of being the conduit that God intended, the man thought it all belonged to him. The love of money representing personal greed kept him from following Christ.

Nothing happens in the economy of God until you give something away. It is a universal law of God. Paul very appropriately reminds us: "Remember this: Whoever sows sparingly will also reap sparingly, and whoever sows generously will also reap generously" (II Corinthians 9:6).

Giving is the trigger for God's financial miracles. When you give to the Kingdom of God, it will be given back to you. But where will it come from? Who will give to you? Will God cause money to float down from heaven so that your needs will be met? No. The Bible says, "shall men give into your ....(life)." This is how the cycle of blessing works.

When you give to God, He in turn causes others to give to you. Perhaps it will be in the form of new customers to your business, new products to sell, and so on. When God owns your business, He will make sure it prospers.

The Scriptures illustrate that giving of one's own things is an evidence of God's grace in a person's life. (II Corinthians 8:4-7) Because 100 percent of what is received comes from God, we are responsible to use it wisely and in accordance with God's will. Like every other area of stewardship, God is interested in the whole picture, not just a percentage. What a person does with all his treasure is important to God.

The Good Samaritan was a trustee of God's provision. The person who takes stewardship seriously will regard his or her life, talents, strength and money as a trust from God. Trustees have specific responsibilities. They are charged with "holding property in trust" for someone else.

Scriptural principles give us clues as to how we can trust God with our money and our entire life. The first step in becoming trustworthy is to faithfully return the tithe to its rightful owner. The tenth belongs to God.

Become a faithful tither today, and this path will take you from obedience to the wonderful blessings of God.

Source Material

21 Unbreakable Laws of Success, Max Anders, Thomas Nelson, 1996

A Christian Guide to Prosperity; Fries & Taylor, California: Communications Research, 1984

A Look At Stewardship, Word Aflame Publications, 2001

American Savings Education Council (http://www.asec.org)

Anointed For Business, Ed Silvoso, Regal, 2002

Avoiding Common Financial Mistakes, Ron Blue, Navpress, 1991

Baker Encyclopedia of the Bible; Walter Elwell, Michigan: Baker Book House, 1988

Becoming The Best, Barry Popplewell, England: Gower Publishing Company Limited, 1988

Business Proverbs, Steve Marr, Fleming H. Revell, 2001

Cheapskate Monthly, Mary Hunt

Commentary on the Old Testament; Keil-Delitzsch, Michigan: Eerdmans Publishing, 1986

Crown Financial Ministries, various publications

Customers As Partners, Chip Bell, Texas: Berrett-Koehler Publishers, 1994

Cut Your Bills in Half; Pennsylvania: Rodale Press, Inc., 1989

Debt-Free Living, Larry Burkett, Dimensions, 2001

Die Broke, Stephen M. Pollan & Mark Levine, HarperBusiness, 1997

Double Your Profits, Bob Fifer, Virginia: Lincoln Hall Press, 1993

Eerdmans' Handbook to the Bible, Michigan: William B. Eerdmans Publishing Company, 1987

Eight Steps to Seven Figures, Charles B. Carlson, Double Day, 2000

Everyday Life in Bible Times; Washington DC: National Geographic Society, 1967

Financial Dominion, Norvel Hayes, Harrison House, 1986

Financial Freedom, Larry Burkett, Moody Press, 1991

Financial Freedom, Patrick Clements, VMI Publishers, 2003

Financial Peace, Dave Ramsey, Viking Press, 2003

Financial Self-Defense; Charles Givens, New York: Simon And Schuster, 1990

Flood Stage, Oral Roberts, 1981

Generous Living, Ron Blue, Zondervan, 1997

Get It All Done, Tony and Robbie Fanning, New York: Pennsylvania: Chilton Book, 1979

Getting Out of Debt, Howard Dayton, Tyndale House, 1986

Getting Out of Debt, Mary Stephenson, Fact Sheet 436, University of Maryland Cooperative Extension Service, 1988

Giving and Tithing, Larry Burkett, Moody Press, 1991

God's Plan For Giving, John MacArthur, Jr., Moody Press, 1985

God's Will is Prosperity, Gloria Copeland, Harrison House, 1978

Great People of the Bible and How They Lived; New York: Reader's Digest, 1974

How Others Can Help You Get Out of Debt; Esther M. Maddux, Circular 759-3,

How To Make A Business Plan That Works, Henderson, North Island Sound Limited, 1989

How To Manage Your Money, Larry Burkett, Moody Press, 1999

How to Personally Profit From the Laws of Success, Sterling Sill, NIFP, Inc., 1978

How to Plan for Your Retirement; New York: Corrigan & Kaufman, Longmeadow Press, 1985

Is God Your Source?, Oral Roberts, 1992

It's Not Luck, Eliyahu Goldratt, Great Barrington, MA: The North River Press, 1994

Jesus CEO, Laurie Beth Jones, Hyperion, 1995

John Avanzini Answers Your Questions About Biblical Economics, Harrison House, 1992

Living on Less and Liking It More, Maxine Hancock, Chicago, Illinois: Moody Press, 1976

Making It Happen; Charles Conn, New Jersey: Fleming H. Revell Company, 1981

Master Your Money Or It Will Master You, Arlo E. Moehlenpah, Doing Good Ministries, 1999

Master Your Money; Ron Blue, Tennessee: Thomas Nelson, Inc. 1986

Miracle of Seed Faith, Oral Roberts, 1970

Mississippi State University Extension Service

Money, Possessions, and Eternity, Randy Alcorn, Tyndale House, 2003

More Than Enough, David Ramsey, Penguin Putnam Inc, 2002

Moving the Hand of God, John Avanzini, Harrison House, 1990

Multiplication, Tommy Barnett, Creation House, 1997

NebFacts, Nebraska Cooperative Extension

New York Post

One Up On Wall Street; New York: Peter Lynch, Simon And Schuster, 1989

Personal Finances, Larry Burkett, Moody Press, 1991

Portable MBA in Finance and Accounting; Livingstone, Canada: John Wiley & Sons, Inc., 1992

Principle-Centered Leadership, Stephen R. Covey, New York: Summit Books, 1991

Principles of Financial Management, Kolb & DeMong, Texas: Business Publications, Inc., 1988

Rapid Debt Reduction Strategies, John Avanzini, HIS Publishing, 1990

Real Wealth, Wade Cook, Arizona: Regency Books, 1985

See You At The Top, Zig Ziglar, Louisianna: Pelican
    Publishing Company, 1977

Seed-Faith Commentary on the Holy Bible, Oral Roberts,
    Pinoak Publications, 1975

Sharkproof, Harvey Mackay, New York: HarperCollins
    Publishers, 1993

Smart Money, Ken and Daria Dolan, New York: Random
    House, Inc., 1988

Strong's Concordance, Tennessee: Crusade Bible Publishers,
    Inc.,

Success by Design, Peter Hirsch, Bethany House, 2002

Success is the Quality of your Journey, Jennifer James, New
    York: Newmarket Press, 1983

Swim with the Sharks Without Being Eaten Alive, Harvey
    Mackay, William Morrow , 1988

The Almighty and the Dollar; Jim McKeever, Oregon: Omega
    Publications, 1981

The Challenge, Robert Allen, New York: Simon And Schuster,
    1987

The Family Financial Workbook, Larry Burkett, Moody Press,
    2002

The Management Methods of Jesus, Bob Briner, Thomas
    Nelson, 1996

The Millionaire Next Door, Thomas Stanley & William Danko,
    Pocket Books, 1996

The Money Book for Kids, Nancy Burgeson, Troll
Associates,1992

The Money Book for King's Kids; Harold E. Hill, New Jersey:
Fleming H. Revell Company, 1984

The Seven Habits of Highly Effective People, Stephen
Covey, New York: Simon And Schuster, 1989

The Wealthy Barber, David Chilton, California: Prima
Publishing, 1991

Theological Wordbook of the Old Testament, Chicago,
Illinois: Moody Press, 1981

Treasury of Courage and Confidence, Norman Vincent Peale,
New York: Doubleday & Co., 1970

True Prosperity, Dick Iverson, Bible Temple Publishing, 1993

Trust God For Your Finances, Jack Hartman, Lamplight
Publications, 1983

University of Georgia Cooperative Extension Service, 1985

Virginia Cooperative Extension

Webster's Unabridged Dictionary, Dorset & Baber, 1983

What Is an Entrepreneur; David Robinson, MA: Kogan Page
Limited, 1990

Word Meanings in the New Testament, Ralph Earle,
Michigan: Baker Book House, 1986

Word Pictures in the New Testament; Robertson, Michigan:
Baker Book House, 1930

Word Studies in the New Testament; Vincent, New York:
Charles Scribner's Sons, 1914

Worth

You Can Be Financially Free, George Fooshee, Jr., 1976, Fleming H. Revell Company.

Your Key to God's Bank, Rex Humbard, 1977

Your Money Counts, Howard, Dayton, Tyndale House, 1997

Your Money Management, MaryAnn Paynter, Circular 1271, University of Illinois Cooperative Extension Service, 1987.

Your Money Matters, Malcolm MacGregor, Bethany Fellowship, Inc., 1977

Your Road to Recovery, Oral Roberts, Oliver Nelson, 1986

Comment On Sources

Over the years I have collected bits and pieces of interesting material, written notes on sermons I've heard, jotted down comments on financial articles I've read, and gathered a lot of great information. It is unfortunate that I didn't record the sources of all of these notes in my earlier years. I gratefully extend my appreciation to the many writers, authors, teachers and pastors from whose articles and sermons I have gleaned much insight.

Rich Brott

Online Resources

American Savings Education Council (http://www.asec.org)

Bloomberg.com (http://www.bloomberg.com)

Bureau of the Public Debt Online (http://www.publicdebt. treas.gov)

BusinessWeek (http://www.businessweek.com)

Charles Schwab & Co., Inc. (http://www.schwab.com)

Consumer Federation of America (http://www. consumerfed.org)

Debt Advice.org (http://www.debtadvice.org)

Federal Reserve System (http://www.federalreserve.gov)

Fidelity Investments (http://www.fidelity.com)

Financial Planning Association (http://www.fpanet.org)

Forbes (www.forbes.com)

Fortune Magazine (http://www.fortune.com)

Generous Giving (http://www.generousgiving.org/)

Investing for Your Future (http://www.investing.rutgers. edu)

Kiplinger Magazine (http://www.kiplinger.com/)

Money Magazine (http://money.cnn.com)

MorningStar (http://www.morningstar.com)

MSN Money (http://moneycentral.msn.com)

Muriel Siebert (http://www.siebertnet.com)

National Center on Education and the Economy
(http://www.ncee.org)

National Foundation for Credit Counseling
(http://www.nfcc.org)

Quicken (http://www.quicken.com)

Smart Money (http://www.smartmoney.com)

Social Security Online (http://www.ssa.gov)

Standard & Poor's (http://www2.standardandpoors.com)

The Dollar Stretcher, Gary Foreman,
(http://www.stretcher.com)

The Vanguard Group (http://flagship.vanguard.com)

U.S. Securities and Exchange Commission
(http://www.sec.gov)

Yahoo! Finance (http://finance.yahoo.com)

Magazine Resources

Business Week

Consumer Reports

Forbes

Kiplinger's Personal Finance

Money

Smart Money

US News and World Report

Newspaper Resources

Barrons

Investors Business Daily

USA Today

Wall Street Journal

Washington Times

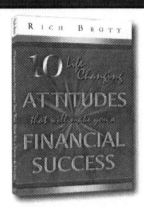

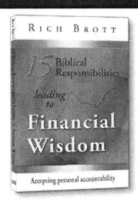

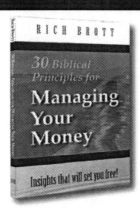

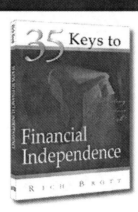

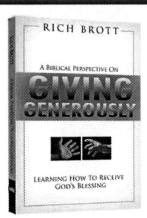

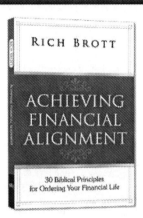

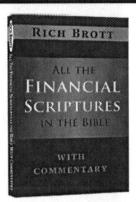

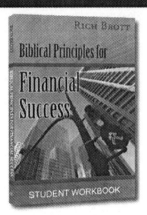

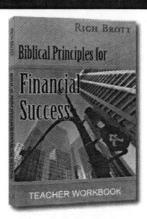

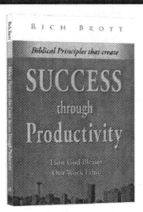

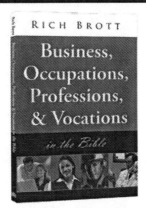

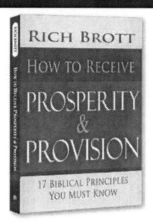

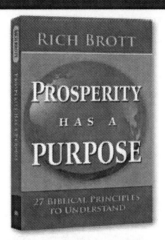

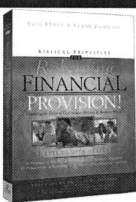

Additional Resources *by Rich Brott*

www.RichBrott.com

Also look for these new titles:

Advancing a Successful Business

Developing a Successful Personal and Business Vision

Establishing a Successful Business

Maximizing Business Success

Book Publishing

www.AbcBookPublishing.com

Printed in the United States
200734BV00018B/178-288/A